Editor-in-Chief and Founder:
Lyndon H. LaRouche, Jr.
Editorial Board: *Lyndon H. LaRouche, Jr. , Helga Zepp-LaRouche, Robert Ingraham, Tony Papert, Gerald Rose, Dennis Small, Jeffrey Steinberg, William Wertz*
Co-Editors: *Robert Ingraham, Tony Papert*
Technology: *Marsha Freeman*
Books: *Katherine Notley*
Ebooks: *Richard Burden*
Graphics: *Alan Yue*
Photos: *Stuart Lewis*
Circulation Manager: *Stanley Ezrol*

INTELLIGENCE DIRECTORS
Counterintelligence: *Jeffrey Steinberg, Michele Steinberg*
Economics: *John Hoefle, Marcia Merry Baker, Paul Gallagher*
History: *Anton Chaitkin*
Ibero-America: *Dennis Small*
Russia and Eastern Europe: *Rachel Douglas*
United States: *Debra Freeman*

INTERNATIONAL BUREAUS
Bogotá: *Miriam Redondo*
Berlin: *Rainer Apel*
Copenhagen: *Tom Gillesberg*
Houston: *Harley Schlanger*
Lima: *Sara Madueño*
Melbourne: *Robert Barwick*
Mexico City: *Gerardo Castilleja Chávez*
New Delhi: *Ramtanu Maitra*
Paris: *Christine Bierre*
Stockholm: *Ulf Sandmark*
United Nations, N.Y.C.: *Leni Rubinstein*
Washington, D.C.: *William Jones*
Wiesbaden: *Göran Haglund*

ON THE WEB
e-mail: eirns@larouchepub.com
www.larouchepub.com
www.executiveintelligencereview.com
www.larouchepub.com/eiw
Webmaster: *John Sigerson*
Assistant Webmaster: *George Hollis*
Editor, Arabic-language edition: *Hussein Askary*

EIR (ISSN 0273-6314) *is published weekly (50 issues), by EIR News Service, Inc., P.O. Box 17390, Washington, D.C. 20041-0390. (703) 297-8434*

European Headquarters: E.I.R. GmbH, Postfach Bahnstrasse 9a, D-65205, Wiesbaden, Germany
Tel: 49-611-73650
Homepage: http://www.eir.de
e-mail: info@eir.de
Director: Georg Neudecker

Montreal, Canada: 514-461-1557
eir@eircanada.ca

Denmark: EIR - Danmark, Sankt Knuds Vej 11, basement left, DK-1903 Frederiksberg, Denmark.
Tel.: +45 35 43 60 40, Fax: +45 35 43 87 57. e-mail: eirdk@hotmail.com.

Mexico City: EIR, Sor Juana Inés de la Cruz 242-2 Col. Agricultura C.P. 11360
Delegación M. Hidalgo, México D.F.
Tel. (5525) 5318-2301
eirmexico@gmail.com

Canada Post Publication Sales Agreement #40683579

Postmaster: Send all address changes to *EIR*, P.O. Box 17390, Washington, D.C. 20041-0390.

Signed articles in *EIR* represent the views of the authors, and not necessarily those of the Editorial Board.

Breakthrough Against Geopolitics

A Racist by Any Other Name ...
Would Stink Like Obama and Bush

Jan. 14—As almost everyone in America—and most of the rest of the world—has heard, on Thursday, Jan. 11, at a closed-door private White House meeting, President Trump allegedly made remarks questioning immigration from "s___hole countries," specifically referring to Haiti.

President Trump has denied he made the remark. Nevertheless, the anti-Trump media had a field day. Leading Democrats, including Sen. Dick Durbin and former Vice President Joe Biden have, on cue, jumped in to denounce the President, once again, as a racist.

What is going on here?

The reality is that the ongoing effort to destroy the Trump Presidency through "Russiagate" is now floundering. Within days, or, at most weeks, the American people will have the evidence from the House Intelligence Committee and others, that they have been watching a coup d'état, beginning as early as the summer of 2016, against candidate, and then President Donald Trump—an ongoing coup conducted by the Clinton campaign, corrupt officials in the Justice Department and the FBI, and Barack Obama's intelligence chiefs acting at the behest of British intelligence.

Hence the frantic race now is to falsely paint the President as an irrational madman and a dyed-in-the-wool racist. This is the oligarchy's fallback option, as Russiagate threatens indictments, not of Trump, but of the conspirators in the Department of Justice and elsewhere who sought to reverse the election and destroy his presidency.

The filth of these treasonous operations against the duly elected President is nauseating. First he is accused of being a

cc/Center for American Progress
Sen. Dick Durbin

White House/Pete Souza
Barack Obama

cc/Center for Progress
Joseph Biden

Gage Skidmore
Hillary Clinton

de facto puppet of Russia, then a racist (remember Charlottesville?), then an anti-woman misogynist, then mentally unfit to hold office (threatening use of the 25th Amendment), and now again a racist.

These bile-filled screeds are worthy of nothing but contempt. For sixteen consecutive years under George W. Bush and Barack Obama, America was led by Presidents who committed global mass murder, and implemented economic policies of the most racist and genocidal nature. Where was Joe Biden during all of this? He was Obama's faithful lapdog. Where was Hillary Clinton? Ditto. Where was Dick Durbin? Backing the repeal of Glass-Steagall, and supporting NAFTA and other pro-Wall Street policies.

On the immigration issue, President Trump has repeatedly raised the issue of the entrance of both drugs and drug gangs into the United States as a result of lax immigration policies. This is an absolutely legitimate concern; it is a life-and-death matter for the future of young people in America. Yet, none of Trump's present-day accusers wants to take this on. Why? Because, when Obama was President, his policy was explicitly pro-drug legalization, and it remains so to this day, shared by many of his former underlings.

More important, the whole question of racism, as it is discussed today in the media, is a cynical, willful fraud. What none of Trump's political assassins want to address is that the issue of race today is inseparable from the question of poverty eradication. Martin Luther King understood this decades ago with his organizing for an inter-racial "Poor Peoples' March" on Washington, D.C. This was also the outlook of Hulan Jack, the former Borough President of Manhattan, when he joined with *EIR* founder Lyndon LaRouche in creating the Committee for a New Africa Policy in 1980.

Today, China, through its magnificent Belt and Road Initiative, has not only lifted 700 million of its own people out of poverty, but is currently engaged in tremendous economic projects in Africa, the poorest parts of South and Central America, and other parts of the world. Trump is attempting to work with China, including the possibility of Chinese investment in large-scale infrastructure construction in the United States. Yet, the same people who slander Trump are now howl-

Library of Congress

The April 22, 1968 Poor People's March in Washington, D.C., calling for economic justice, was planned by Martin Luther King before his assassination.

ing about "the Chinese threat," and attempting to return the world to the British geopolitical view that Russia and China are our enemies.

We are not at war with either Russia or China. They are not our enemies. The best course of action for America would be to engage them, work with them, and cooperate on policies of economic development. Pull people out of poverty. Develop the world. And that has been the directionality of the Trump Presidency, despite massive opposition, since the day he took office.

Beginning with the repeal of Glass-Steagall in 1999, followed by the policy of Wall Street bailouts in 2008, and throughout the entirety of the Bush and Obama administrations, America has been raped economically. Poverty rates have skyrocketed, mass homelessness is a reality, suicides go up and up, and an out-of-control drug epidemic claims more and more lives. Financial speculators, con-artists, gamblers, and the one percent billionaires have luxuriated in their wealth. Bush and Obama are their pals. Hillary Clinton and her ilk shed crocodile tears for the poor while taking millions from Wall Street criminals.

To this day, George W. Bush defends his "record," Barack Obama defends his record, and almost all who served under them chime in. These are the people— with guidance from Britain—who now seek to destroy the Trump presidency. Why would anyone listen to these liars, murderers and criminals?

This is a war. Pick your side and fight.

EIR Contents

www.larouchepub.com Volume 45, Number 3, January 19, 2018

*Cover
This Week*

Terracotta Army detail, Xi'an China.

cc/Peter Morgan

BREAKTHROUGH AGAINST GEOPOLITICS

I. French President Visits China

French President Emmanuel Macron, calling on the legacy of President De Gaulle's bold move to challenge the Malthusian, British empire cold war geopolitical lunacy, brought a diplomatic and business mission to China, January 8-10. DeGaulle, in 1964, had shocked the lunacy of that nuclear-unhinged post-JFK world, by officially recognizing the People's Republic of China and most importantly by speaking to the universal values of humanity, reflected in universal history, saying, "It is not to be excluded that China will once again, during the next century, become what it was throughout the centuries, the greatest power of the Universe."

Macron began his trip on the morning of Jan. 8 with a visit to the Silk Road gateway of Xi'an. We present his speech here. That speech was followed in the afternoon by a meeting with Chinese President Xi Jinping in Beijing and a state dinner. Macron discussed his China trip with President Donald Trump, before his departure and upon his return, according to official reports from the White House and the Elysée, the French presidential headquarters.

JACQUES CHEMINADE

France's Macron Joins 'Common Fight' with China, for Peace and Mutual Development of Mankind

The following is an edited transcript, translated from the original French, of the interview with Jacques Cheminade on **RT France**, *on the morning of Jan. 9, 2018. The full video interview, titled, "Multilateral Cooperation or Wall Street: Macron has to choose, according to Jacques Cheminade," is available at* https://youtu.be/sGP1E-F4kHGY

RT: This morning, we welcome Jacques Cheminade, founder of the Solidarité et Progrès Party. Good morning, Mr. Cheminade.

Cheminade: Good morning.

RT: Thank you for having accepted our invitation.

All photos courtesy of RT France

Jacques Cheminade, on left, during interview presented here by RT France. President of France Emmanuel Macron, on right, speaking in Xi'an, China, Jan. 8.

First, about Emmanuel Macron's gift of a horse[1] to his Chinese counterpart, Xi Jinping, what do you make of

---

1. The horse, Vesuvius, had been part of the French presidential cavalry.

Shown at right, French President Macron is greeted upon arrival by Chinese Foreign Minister Wang Yi.

it? What are your thoughts on this "horse diplomacy"?

Cheminade: This is very interesting. They say in Chinese that a name is an arrangement of things; that Emmanuel Macron's name is related to "the horse which accompanies the dragon."[2]

RT: "…which tames the dragon."

Cheminade: Yes, they say "which tames the dragon." But Macron has been a bit more of a charmer. In his Xi'an speech he referred to the panda given to him by China, whose name, Yuang Meng, means the "accomplishment of a dream" and concluded, "We are living at a time when China and France can afford to dream together." So, this is where we start from; we start from his visit which begins in Xi'an, which is the door to the Silk Road, and also Xi'an is the region where President Xi Jinping comes from.[3]

RT: Don't you think that Macron is encroaching on your turf? He goes to China and he defends this great project of yours, the New Silk Road, which you had espoused during the 2017 French presidential elections.

Cheminade: In 1994-95, I championed the conception of a New Silk Road, which would permit the creation of a stable system of cooperation and mutual development in the world. And with that, we then could move to a still greater project, to go further than that, to create a Worldwide Land-Bridge, to secure peace.

RT: So you are going further with the idea. Emmanuel Macron mentioned that great project with Xi Jinping and strongly put Europe up front, with the idea of a Brussels-Beijing axis, presenting himself as the leader of Europe in China, as the promoter of the new Silk Road project. How do you see your role in this development, Mr. Cheminade?

Cheminade: I think that what French President Macron said is very important: "We are the memory of the world and it is our responsibility to decide if we are going to be its future." This is how he ended his presentation in Xi'an. This is very important.

---

2. In China, French President Macron was given a surname which the

Chinese pronounce "Ma-Ke-Long," and which the French media have translated into "the horse which tames the dragon."

3. Xi'an is also home to the world famous archeological site of the Terra Cotta Warriors and Horses.

He said that the Silk Road—actually there are seven New Silk Roads, they are corridors which generate development. They are not merely axes of transportation; this is a civilizational undertaking. Today, I am tempted to quote the poem by Aragon:

When wheat is under hail
Fool is he who is frets like a delicate flower.
Fools are they who think of their quarrels
In the midst of a common fight...[4]

And, for me, this common fight comes down to two things. First is the need to restore peace in the world by way of mutual development. The New Silk Roads belong to this world-view, which is the perspective of this win-win system that Xi Jinping is talking about. Second is the fight against this greedy and predatory financial system of the City of London and Wall Street. Obviously, Emmanuel Macron will have to make a choice: either he goes entirely in the direction of what he defined in China, or he lays out the red carpet for London and Wall Street. He cannot have both at the same time. He has to make a choice.

RT: This New Silk Road project, is it a bilateral relationship here? There is no mention of Russia from Macron. But you have spoken about Russia as being part of that development.

Cheminade: Yes, Russia is a part. French Finance Minister Bruno Le Maire went to Moscow on Dec. 19, and he was interviewed by the *Wall Street Journal*. He said that he totally opposed what the American Congress had decided, adopting an extra-territorial judicial approach of imposing sanctions. The world is now turning toward the East and it is necessary for France to play a role, not by excluding the United States, but to have a vision which goes toward mutual development. He spoke about a Paris-Moscow-Beijing commercial axis. Emmanuel Macron did not mention it on the China trip; it was probably not the right moment, but he nevertheless said clearly that it was absolutely necessary that there be a policy of cooperation extending beyond France and China, and that France and China could set the ex-

Xinhua/Wang Ye

President of China Xi Jinping

President Macron and First Lady visit the Forbidden City, Jan. 9, 2018.

ample, beyond their respective borders in the world. This is also what Xi Jinping has said, on several occasions, saying, "We don't want to impose our system on others, and we don't want others to impose their system

---

4. "La rose et le réséda" by Louis Aragon (1897-1982), written in his role as a unifying force in the French resistance to the Nazis.

on us." And their system, the Chinese system of today, is socialism with Chinese characteristics.

RT: At the same time, Emmanuel Macron issued a warning against some sort of hegemony. What sort of "hegemony" is he talking about?

Cheminade: He did not precisely say that. He said that all along the Silk Road, people should not take the opportunity to create new forms of subjugation. He said it because that's what he meant. But I don't think it is in the Chinese vision, today. Yes, in the Silk Road, there is a desire to establish China as a great universal power, but as General de Gaulle spoke about in 1964—when he recognized the People's Republic of China. However, the Chinese do have a sense that their own interest is also the interest of others, which is the basis of the idea of a win-win system. And Emmanuel Macron showed that he had an understanding of this when he said that the New Silk Roads were reactivating the power of imagination of civilization for the future, and this future is for the whole world to share. And I believe that all of this pertains to what Charles De Gaulle had called "détente, entente and cooperation." It remains to be defined and it won't be easy, but Macron said that we have to progress together, even if we are "in the dark and moving forward warily." I really like that expression.

RT: So, one last question. What should we pay attention to from Emmanuel Macron's trip to China? His visit is not over yet, and there are a lot of contracts at stake in the offing. What about the reinforcement of the economic partnership with Beijing?

Cheminade: Pay attention to the nuclear agreements, the digital and artificial intelligence domain, and cooper-

ation in food and agriculture, in addition to the policy on aging and employment, China's version of the Résidence pour Personnes Agées (RPA), which is an excellent institution for retirement homes, plus the fight to restore an environment which would favor progress and the improvement of life in urban centers.

So, there is all of that, but at the same time, there is Civilization. We have to understand that China, notably under the Song Dynasty of the North, a long time ago, had the largest capital city in the world, Kaifeng, with one million people. So, we have to understand all of that history. That history is part of this concept of Civilization. We have to understand, at the same time that we have also to, as Emmanuel Macron would say, go toward what Russia represents, between China and Europe. We already know what Leibniz did in the 17th Century.

Today, all of this is being concretized by the fact that Emmanuel Macron will be the guest of honor at the Saint Petersburg Forum in May. Therefore, what we are looking at is a change of manifold, and I think that the Russian authorities, and particularly President Putin, are beginning to understand—which was not necessarily the case during the French elections—that there is in France a strong Gaullist presence, a patriotic orientation, which transcends parties.

I think that this is what transpired during Macron's trip to China, there's that. And I, like France, would hope to be a catalyst in the world, a very small thing which assures that a chemical reaction works; that is, peace in the world, development, or peace through development. What I wish to be is a catalytic means of a very small thing, which in France would reorient politics toward that process of change which Emmanuel Macron has opened in China, but in which he did not go far enough. Therefore, one more time: One cannot be at the same time a partner in this policy of multilateral cooperation on the one side, and serve the financial system of the City of London and of Wall Street on the other.

RT: Thank you very much, Jacques Cheminade, President of the Solidarité et Progrès Party, and former presidential candidate in the last French presidential elections. Thank you for this visit.

Cheminade: Thank you.

The New Silk Roads of China, a New Meaning And a New Language Towards a Renewed World Order and Dream for Humanity

This is an edited speech, parts of which are paraphrased, that French President Emmanuel Macron delivered in Xi'an, China, Jan. 8.

Macron began:

"I am very happy today to have the opportunity to speak to you after having spent the morning with you, my hosts, in this beautiful city of Xi'an.

"France has, for a very long time, seen itself in the mirror of China. China has brought together, over the centuries, profound ideas, poetry and art, as well as reflections on war, power, and human existence. China has invigorated our imagination with ambitious voyages, carrying extraordinary merchandise and singular discoveries.

"It is the China of merchants, discovered by Marco Polo—and the treasures that followed from a civilization that seemed mysterious and was poorly understood, which traveled on those Silk Roads, to which you give, today, a new meaning and a new language. Today we must remember, in our imagination, those caravans arriving at the oasis of Dunhuang with the treasure of your civilization echoing in the sand dunes.

"The shipments of foodstuffs and merchandise that were exchanged were accompanied by thoughts, words, and customs—a type of phenomenon noted by Marguerite Yourcenar in her fictional *Memoirs of Hadrian*—which would rapidly take over the globe, faster than marching legions. They brought back from their wanderings unknown objects and materials in which France and other countries immediately delighted, not in a faddish ephemeral way, but with the intensity of a discovery that became integrated into our historical culture. There is hardly a royal castle today that doesn't have a Chinese salon, hardly an artist, artisan or engineer who has not been fascinated by the styles and techniques learned from China.

"This continues in our times, because China is the country of inventors and engineers who are constantly inventing the future. China is also its broad diaspora spread throughout the world, progressively transform-

Xinhua/Liu Xiao

French President Emmanuel Macron and the First Lady are hosted at China's cultural treasure, the Terracotta Warriors and Horses of Emperor Qin Shihuang in Xi'an, Jan. 8, 2018.

ing the cities in which they live. France is honored to have the largest Chinese diaspora in Europe.

"It is the China of warriors that I just witnessed in the Xi'an terracotta army necropolis—which forms part of the respect for the figure of the Chinese soldier, a soldier immortalized by Sun Tzu in his book, *The Art of War*, which has been known to Europeans since the 18th century, and which is still used with students in our military schools.

"We share this same respect for soldiers, the honors due to soldiers and those others who die in service for their country. I pay tribute here to all your compatriots, buried in the French Nolette Chinese Cemetery in the Somme, which is dear to me, or in other places. Most of them were not soldiers, but Chinese workers who came to support France's effort during the First World War.

"Thousands were assigned to difficult tasks in mines, trenches, or factories, working with soldiers and the sick—with the French people. Some went on to start families, others left. Many are with us today in France. A few months before the commemoration of the end of that world conflict, I want us to remember them; they were our brothers in those tragic hours.

"It is also the China of writers and thinkers; it is almost 450 years since the founding of first Jesuit mission in China.

"We, the French people, never cease to examine and question. From the beginning, we perceived in the Chinese way of thinking a vision of the world, anchored in beliefs and concepts different than ours. We have, for more than 200 years, seen differences with the seeming basis of our own beliefs, And yet, in this very difference, we also believe in a human community, because often this difference is convergence. Poets have the best feel for this. So is your poet Wang Bo, from whom one can understand you, even at the opposite end of the world, like a neighbor. Or Victor Segalen, who came to China to find the bricks and tiles of his poetry, and discovering here, in Xi'an, the faded but rich smell of buried centuries."

He continued by describing the impact of Chinese literature and poetry on the writings of Paul Claudel and Saint-John Perse, and praised the translators, "who tirelessly translate, question, and publish our literature." Macron asserted, "Nothing can replace this fruitful contact between our two languages, our two universes, our cultures, and a constant proof that dialogue is possible."

He continued, saying:

"Sometimes, when those of us from Europe try to understand China, to forge a path to understanding, we are often told that it's an incomprehensible continent. Don't expect to come back to China; there are too many opposing groups."

He explained, "I do not believe in this attitude, for all the reasons I just mentioned. There are things which are untranslatable, chasms that we must narrow, but there are always ways and paths, to gradually circumscribe these untranslatable things and find the paths that bind us. The Chinese culture, like the French culture, must be apprehended in all of its historical nuances," and praised, by name, each of the great French Sinologists, students of Chinese geography, of intellectual, political, and artistic culture.

Macron continued:

"Sinology in Europe was born in France. In the Nineteenth Century philosophers and historians always turned to the French experts to try to understand China. This has always been a fruitful dialogue, and one we must always approach with humility. It was a unique position. When Europeans, for decades, wanted to understand China, they went to a French Sinologist, and very often, when the Chinese wanted to go to Europe, to understand it intimately, they went through the same route, through France.

"European Sinology continues to reinvent itself today in France, and remains a key discipline in our intellectual landscape. Inalco, the French National Institute of Oriental Languages and Civilizations, has been a vital element for more than two centuries. We must remember that there will be detours, that we need humility, because dialogue can be sometimes long and difficult. Always, we must have respect, to enrich our mutual fascination and friendly curiosity, and there find a path.

"Our history shows that we are always enriched by our differences; whether visually, through harmonies, or by the spoken word, we have always found a path for exchanges. We find beautiful what you find beautiful. I speak here from this imperial palace of Daminggong, cradle of the Tang Dynasty and many high points of your art, your history. France renews the commitment, begun in 2016, to work with you to preserve these treasures of mankind.

"We share a deep sense of the history of the world and its people, and it is not to be taken lightly that we find that certain places, and their sense of universal value, equally important and beautiful. With that commonality, we have had a great friendship that endures beyond the tangled paths of unfolding events. General de Gaulle spoke about 'the choice of reason,' but also 'the choice of the evidence,' in his 1964 decision to grant diplomatic recognition to the People's Republic of China. It is this evidence today that is still the hallmark; the evidence of a relationship of centuries, the evidence of a joint concern to apprehend the world in its complexity, the evidence of a shared future in today's mutual concerns."

"France and China are not only two nations," Macron said, "but two civilizations," because both share a certain conception of man. Humanity is today at a crossroads, and its future is at stake, and in this context, China and France "have a common destiny." The key notions around which this relationship must be built are "three: intelligence, justice, and balance."

Intelligence

"We need shared intelligence to create a better world and to fight all forms of obscurantism: Islamic terrorism, blind nationalism," which lead to war, isolationism, a vain attempt to protect oneself from the world. Intelligence to overcome fears "which exist in Europe against China. In one generation you had the energy to become one of the main world powers and now you have the ambition to go beyond. The rapidity of that change can provoke fears. . . . The only way to overcome them is to work to understand what the word 'power' means for each of us."

By intelligence, he means more education for all the citizens, but also a joint partnership in digital technologies and artificial intelligence. China has 37 million university students, the Confucius Institutes, artists, massive investment in new, digital technologies and artificial intelligence. France is also moving in that direction. "Even though we are known here for our art of living, gastronomy, and romanticism, we are also a digital power, with energy transition, artificial intelligence, innovation, research, industry, a financial industry," emphasized Macron.

We will be stronger if we lead this fight for "intelligence" together, he stressed, proposing first to multiply cultural projects such as the permanent exhibit on the Han Dynasty at the Paris Asian museum, Musée Guimet. Macron also proposed the creation of "a great

Exhibit at the Paris Asian art museum, Musée Guimet.

European Sinology institute," and the founding of new partnerships on innovation, digital, and technologies. For this we need numerous creative individuals, and free innovation. The strength of your country is that you have millions of people who are creative individuals. We also need partnerships in energy transition, medical innovation, and innovation in agriculture and food industries, to ensure our food sovereignty. The teaching of languages must also be encouraged, particularly in French.

Justice in the Crisis of Global Capitalism

The second pillar, is the fight for justice, and first of all, social justice, said Macron, recognizing that China has succeeded in pulling some 700 million out of poverty in the last decades.

This is a challenge for France, confronted by mass unemployment, but also the whole world is undergoing a crisis of globalized capitalism which has led to an explosion of inequalities and to the concentration of wealth, over the last ten years.

Joint Development in Africa

To overcome France's history of "unilateral imperialism in Africa," Macron proposed that France and China work together in Africa, where China has invested a lot in recent years in infrastructure, in raw materials, with strong financial support that European nations don't have. But France has a historical and cultural knowledge of Africa which are important for the future. He called on launching joint, financially sustainable projects in Africa which are very useful for the growth of the continent, without reproducing the errors of the past, i.e., creating financial and political dependence under the pretext of development. Tomorrow the Agence Française de Développement and the China Development Bank will sign a contract on this basis. "France's history of unilateral imperialism sometimes lead to the worst results." Today, with the launching of these New Silk Roads, a partnership between France and China can avoid those errors.

Macron invited China to join the conference on partnership in education that France is organizing next February in Dakar, Senegal, and so to give another face to those Silk Roads where immense work has been done in infrastructures and economic development.

Balance

Finally, the last pillar: Macron called for reaching a balance, a kind of new world order from which China will no longer be excluded.

The histories of both countries have been sometimes made of "tensions," of "periods of hegemony," and of "imperial wills, each in its own manner, maritime or continental," he recognized, stating, however that what unites France and China is their connection to the world, their claim to universality.

"We live in a world where stability was established more than 60 years ago, at the end of one of the worst conflicts the world has ever seen, when barbarism struck at the heart of Europe.

"We structured globalization with a notion of in-

Presidency of the French Republic

Senegal President Macky Sall (right) with President of France Emmanuel Macron.

ternational law and international structures of which China is at the heart, like us, as a permanent member of the Security Council, but where I know China sometimes has the feeling of having been left outside," a feeling that "this postwar order is a Western order not really made for us. And sometimes the Western powers have contributed to develop that sentiment."

"We are living today through a crisis of this contemporary world order which has been weakened by the emergence of authoritarian powers, because nuclear proliferation has re-emerged as a threat and because contemporary capitalism is being overwhelmed by its own excess and is producing the social inequalities I alluded to earlier or the climate inequalities we're experiencing."

In this context, Macron raised the geopolitical problems in the world, such as North Korea, international terrorism, and the Middle East. On the Korean crisis, he praised China's contribution to solving the problem. He committed France to a negotiated solution to the crisis. In the fight against terrorism, he said that he expects terrorism to rebound in Asia, after having been eliminated in the Middle East. On these questions, Macron apologized for the role of France and the West in the destabilizations of Libya and Iraq, and committed himself never to use force against sovereign nations.

"From Central Asia to Southern Asia, there are numerous threats which can weaken the entire continent.

It is therefore our responsibility to fight together against them, building political solutions to the conflicts and drawing the lessons of past errors. I want to say this very clearly: I think there must be a community of views concerning how to solve those conflicts. In each country where divisions exist, where authoritarian regimes are deployed, where sometimes the worst is on hand, France will not defend military solutions which will act against people's sovereignty. We will do everything to work with civil societies and with our friends to bring about pluralist political solutions that will allow all people at the same time to respect one another, to eradicate terrorism, and also to build durable political solutions."

He continued: "We must draw the lessons of past errors. Every time we tried to impose the truth or the law against the people themselves, we were wrong and sometimes even produced worse situations. Such was Iraq, or Libya today. We need to work together to develop the respect of sovereignty of all people...." He expressed the wish in this respect that both can work together toward "inclusive" political solutions in Libya or in Syria in the coming months, and called for a common fight against the sources of terrorist financing. There will be a conference in Paris in April on that very subject, which is open to China as well.

"Multilateralism must be redefined, based on this new idea of balance that we now share. Some in China say that the rules presiding over international relations have been written thus far by the West. To that I respond very soberly that history sets a frame but does not necessarily impose it upon us. Our two millenary nations have survived because we were always able to reinvent ourselves, despite sometimes being victimized by the history often invented by us, and we were also able to accept difficult periods, but also to seize the opportunities to grow and shine."

Harmony Against Geopolitics

"The more important place a country occupies, the greater the responsibilities. The multilateralism which must be redefined implies finding balanced cooperation to be invented for this new century. There should be neither a disguised supremacy, nor a conflict between competing supremacies. All our art, if I can use that word, will not be an art of war but an art of balanced cooperation in order to ensure in the geostrategic, political, and economic levels the harmony our world needs.

"If the multilateralism that we have is challenged and if China wants to engage in this battle, the conclusion is for me very clear. It is up to Europe and Asia, up to France and China, to define and propose together the rules of a game in which we will all win, or we will all lose. I have come thus to tell China my determination to have the Euro-Chinese partnership enter into the 21st century with this new grammar we must all define together. Europe will engage resolutely in this strategy because it is conscious of its role in the century to come."

Europe and the Silk Roads

"Europe is back," claimed Macron, and said that it is so "because some of us want to give it a perspective of medium term, 10 to 15 years, to rebuild a sovereign, united, democratic Europe which will be an economic, social, environmental, and scientific power able to dialogue with China and the U.S." He continued, "We are working with the German Chancellor and number of other European leaders for a project aimed at providing the heart of Europe with the elements of sovereignty, and the year 2018 will be a turning point in this respect. ...

"I want you to understand something today: France is here, becoming transformed in depth and wants to be that country of dialogue and construction of a new partnership for the 21st Century with China. With it, Europe is back and wants, through the building of its own power, to build a balanced cooperation with China in the coming century.

"It is through honest, loyal and readable dialogue that we will be able to progress. ... It is a trust built by trial and error methods. It is to decide to make a step, then another, and that we decide together, and that there is no lasting friendship if it doesn't follow this road. ... It is in this same spirit that I wish for us to advance on those Silk Roads. Indeed, One Belt, One Road is the perspective that China gave itself and that it has proposed to the world. And when a proposal is on the table, it is not my habit not to discuss it. I understand the opportunities for China, on the economic level for finding new markets internationally; on the political level in order to open up regions hit by underdevelopment; on the diplomatic level, to stabilize trade in fragile regions where there are states in difficulty...; on the cultural level since it's a matter of exerting a leadership with the force of new ideas."

The two-unit Taishan nuclear power project, using advanced, third-generation nuclear power technology, under construction in Chixzhen, Taishan, Guangdong province, China. It is a China-foreign joint project with large participation by Areva and Electricité de France. The bulk of French electricity production is nuclear powered. France exports electricity to Germany, which is stupidly shutting down all its nuclear plants by 2022.

The Silk Roads Must Be Shared Roads

"I think that the initiative of the New Silk Roads can meet our interests, those of France and of Europe, if we give ourselves the means to really work together. After all, the Silk Roads were never purely Chinese, to be honest. When we talk about the Maritime Silk Roads they were first Portuguese. On land, they went through Central Asia, Iran, Iraq, Tyre, and Antioch, and in so doing they were Sino-European. The genius of the first Silk Roads was to have reinvented often the European routes to make the Chinese. ... I'm trying to say that those roads are simply essentially the same, those roads are always shared. And if they are routes, they cannot be only one-sided. They must go back and forth."

I Am Ready To Work with the New Silk Road

"I am ready to work on our common objectives. The programs for roads, railways, airports, maritime routes, and technological development along the Silk Roads provide a solution to the deficit in infrastructure, especially in Asia, and creates new perspectives in sectors such as transport, water management, waste, planned cities, and the green economy. Combining our public and private financial resources for trans-border projects can reinforce the connectivity between Europe and Asia, and the Middle East and Africa, contributing to the expansion, integration and coherent structuring of trade and growth of the improvement to come in these regions.

"The city of Xi'an is the living example of how they will be able to do even better. Those first Silk Roads brought Buddhism, Islam and Christianity here. Those roads will lead to cultural and educational exchanges, and to profound transformations in the countries they are crossing. It is a matter of giving ourselves a perspective at a moment when we have lost the excitement of the great epics, which are so cruelly absent in the world. I must say, it is one of the great merits of those Silk Roads proposed by Xi Jinping. Those Silk Roads reactivate the imagination of a new civilization, of fruitful exchanges of shared wealth. They show to all those who thought that we were in a tired, post-modern world, where the great epics were forbidden, that those who decide to live great epics can make the others dream as well. I believe profoundly in great epic stories. It is up to France, and with it, to Europe to contribute its own part of imagination to this proposal and to work at it in the months and years to come. ..."

Speaking of balanced cooperation, he said, "I believe that to progress towards those objectives that we share, we must give ourselves also good rules. ... We must respond to objectives that we assign ourselves as common goods. ... The Silk Roads cannot be the routes of a new hegemonism which would make vassals of the countries they cross. They must contribute to the intelligence of the 21st Century." Among the new rules: those of "transparency, interoperability, opening of public markets, respect of competition, intellectual property, sharing of risks, that we already deal with together in the framework of the G-20. The respect for those principles is obviously essential, simply because they allow for a mutually beneficial partnership, and an increased financial sustainability, and therefore success of the projects engaged. ...

"This will be the object of my exchanges with President Xi Jinping to define the agenda of trust that I hope we can put together.

"I know some will say that this agenda of trust must create equilibrium between a developed country and a developing one. But China is no longer a developing country; it is a country which is largely bypassing that. Therefore, we must reinvent here also the terms of a new relationship, and the Silk Roads are the expression of that new relationship of China to the world.

"I propose to identify very concretely the political framework in which we can build that partnership, that cooperation and common strategy ... I am profoundly convinced that if Europe and China know how to establish that goal together, ... this trust initiative could be the occasion of pragmatically relaunching the multilateralism which is today lacking in concrete accomplishments.

"I am ready to play a key role in this direction, making sure that the European countries progress in unity, because China needs a solid interlocutor to exchange and build its own initiative. I want the Silk Roads not to be limited to economic questions, but to be enlightened in Europe by a deep comprehension of China.

www.elysee

President Macron, speaking at the Daming Palace in Xi'an, China, Jan. 8.

All the resources must be used to this end, from the world of publishing to the world of theater and cinema; from the well-recognized pioneering of the French Sinology school, to the world of arts. You have understood it. My outlook is indeed, in that framework, that France and Europe take full responsibility and meet the proposal offered by China."

Macron continued, saying that a few days ago he visited the panda offered by China to Mrs. Macron. Other than the pleasure he and his family got from this gift, he looked closer to see if something there could inspire his trip to China. He didn't have to look for a long time, he said. "His very name enlightened me. The little panda's name is indeed Yuang Meng, 'the realization of a dream.' We live in a world where France and China can allow themselves to dream together."

Macron: I Will Come To China At Least Once A Year

"Trust is built progressively. I also know that the character for wisdom in Chinese, is 'to listen.' Therefore I have decided to adopt a method: To say things as I said them to you today, to try define an objective. We will try to do this with President Xi Jinping, with a clear method of listening, proposing to progress and build confidence.

"At the heart of our two nations, the spirit which will make the world of tomorrow into a world at the level of the challenges of humanity, must grow. It is this spirit that I want to share with you, build with you, construct with you. Our grand past gives us an insatiable taste for the future and this future awaits us. It needs France, Europe, and a China that is respected and listened to. We are the memory of the world; it is up to us to decide to be the future."

French President Macron Joins China's New Silk Road

Helga Zepp-LaRouche's Jan. 11 Webcast can be seen at new-paradigm.schillerinstitute.com. This is an edited transcript.

Harley Schlanger: Hello. I'm Harley Schlanger from the Schiller Institute. Welcome to this week's international strategic webcast with Helga Zepp-LaRouche, the president of the Schiller Institute.

We're again in a situation where there have been some very phenomenal breakthroughs, things which are completely outside of what you would expect, but most of the world is still not hearing about them. Most important was the visit of French President Emmanuel Macron to China. This has enormous implications. Helga, catch us up on what this means.

Xinhua/Wang Ye

China President Xi Jinping (left) at welcoming ceremony for France President Emmanuel Macron, before their talks in Beijing, China.

Helga Zepp-LaRouche: Well, this is a real breakthrough, and I know that many people have different opinions about Macron, but I must say, if somebody goes in the right direction, one should be positive about it. What he did, is he went on a three-day visit to China. He is the first European leader to visit since the 19th Party Congress of the Communist Party of China, and he went to Xi'an first, which is the place where the ancient Silk Road started from the Chinese side, and made a very remarkable speech. And I would urge all interested political people—people who are really trying to get to the truth of the matter—don't believe what you read in the media, just read the speech, here or here.

It's a 1 hour and 15 minute speech, and the fact that he admits some of the most horrible mistakes of Western policy is a reason why I tend to believe that he really is making a change in French policy.

For example: He not only fully endorsed the New Silk Road of China, he called it a "treasure of civilization"; he said we must never repeat the mistakes of the past, such as in Iraq and Libya. He also said he wants to invite China to cooperate with France in projects in Africa, so that France would not repeat the mistakes of the past, of imperial unilateralism in Africa. He said that one must make sure that one does not create new dependencies politically and economically under the pretext of development aid, but that therefore he invites China to participate, because if China and France work

President of France Emmanuel Macron in China.

together on the development of Africa, these mistakes can be avoided.

There were many other elements in his speech: He praised the Chinese policy as creating a great epic, one of the great epics of history. He said, we in the West have become tired, and epics are not allowed any more, but they are exactly what is needed.

I think this is a very, very positive development. On the plane on the way back to Europe, he was asked by reporters, "But what about the tension between the EU and China?" And he said this is not to be blamed on China; it's entirely the fault of the EU.

These sorts of statements really convince me that he means what he says, and I find it highly interesting that shortly after his speech in Xi'an, the EU put out a statement saying that it wants to come forward with its own plan of connectivity intended to be linked up with the Belt and Road Initiative of China. This was welcomed by the Chinese Foreign Ministry, which praised it, saying this means there will be a win-win cooperation to the benefit of both sides.

So, there is a lot going on, and I think this is very positive, because this can only be an inspiration for President Trump, because if even the EU, which has been *really* against this initiative, which it tried to block entirely for years—if even it moves now … Obviously one has to see what they do about financing this, because the famous, or infamous "Juncker plan" for infrastructure, which supposedly had 350 billion euros, never materialized because it was all based on the idea of private investments which never came. Because, ob-

viously, this kind of infrastructure cannot be financed by private capital, but this is something which needs a credit system. And that would mean the EU has to change. It would have to abandon its [zero-deficit] debt brake, which is now in the constitutions of all member-states, and Germany, too, if it were ever to join, would have to abandon the [no-deficit] policy of the so-called "black zero." In fact, Germany just had a budget surplus, I think of 38 billion euros, which is quite a bit. So it could start investing some of this money in these projects, because the infrastructure in Germany is also in a very pitiful condition— let alone other European countries.

This is a breakthrough, and all the various opponents of the New Silk Road, I think they will realize that the Silk Road is there, it's coming, it's spreading, and it is a new paradigm. And I think it's the victorious paradigm, as compared to the outdated neo-liberal model.

Reflections of a Positive Initiative

Schlanger: I think this is absolutely extraordinary. Let me ask something that's important. When you came back from the Belt and Road Forum [in May 2017] you made a very strong point of the fact that the Europeans *must* respond, particularly the Germans. But you said, what's going on with Brussels and Berlin? And now we see this possible move from the European Union.

On the other side, Helga, this is not getting much coverage in the Western press, and what we're seeing now, is that there's a new round of attacks on China. You mentioned that there have been some in the German press. What are they saying?

Zepp-LaRouche: Yes, actually it is quite incredible. Because one day before Macron made this really very excellent speech in Xi'an, there was a long article, I think over four pages in the Sunday edition of the *Frankfurter Allgemeine Zeitung (FAZ)* which is the leading neo-liberal newspaper in Germany. And this is a vitriolic attack, saying China now has a sinister plan, that they are digital communists who are trying to have surveillance of everything, and they go on—it is just absolutely void of any comprehension of the fact that Xi Jinping has, indeed, introduced a completely new paradigm into international politics, based on respect for the other country's social system, respect for the sovereignty, and respect for the UN Charter. And even they cannot avoid mentioning that China has had an unprecedented success story in lifting 800 million people out of poverty in a very short period of time. But then they use that to say that China wants to take over the world. It's just absolutely insane.

And they quote Niall Ferguson, they quote the director of the supposedly expert think tank MERICS—Sebastian Heilmann is his name—to warn in the starkest terms against the sinister intentions of China.

Now, obviously, China is putting healthy pressure on other countries—you cannot maintain, as in Germany, an absolutely exaggerated, green ecologist policy, when China is moving forward in all high-tech areas. One of the most positive developments of the Macron visit to China is that there is now a big agreement to have cooperation in the area of nuclear energy: They are building a reprocessing plant in China together, and some other projects, while Germany foolishly made an exit from nuclear energy, which is really not the way to go. And you can see that the prices of energy are going up in Germany, and driving away all the energy-intensive firms. So what China is doing is putting healthy pressure on some countries.

Also, there is major cooperation in aerospace between France and China, so I think it is a very welcome provocation, and some people are freaking out, including, for example, a program on the German-Swiss-Austrian television network 3sat, which said China is taking over Switzerland. I have not seen this program yet, but I have heard about it. So I think a hysterical reaction is emerging because the Chinese are, indeed, proposing a model which is more attractive, especially to developing countries, than the austerity policy of the EU or the policy of Wall Street, or the policy of the City of London. We will see more of that.

But I'm absolutely convinced that now since the East European, the Central European, the Mediterranean countries, and now also France, Switzerland, and Austria all cooperating, it is only a question of time before it will be clear. And this recent EU statement—even though one has to look at what it says in the fine print—all of these are reflections of the fact that this *is* the only positive strategic initiative on the global agenda, and I think it will win.

Macron's agreements with China impact Europe's extreme environmentalist policy. Shown, an antinuclear demonstration in Berlin.

The Real Issues Facing the U.S.A.

Schlanger: And this is what you have been talking about for a long time, that the new paradigm is unstoppable. I just want to get your thoughts on what's happening in Berlin where now there are ongoing coalition talks. Is any of this being reflected in Germany?

Zepp-LaRouche: Well, if it is reflected, they are trying their very best to hide it, because it has not come out in the open. There was lip service by German Chancellor Merkel, when the G-20 summit took place in Hamburg [in July 2017], that she wants to cooperate with China in some projects in Africa, but nothing has been heard about this since. [Foreign Minister and Vice Chancellor] Gabriel went on record to accuse China of dividing the European Union—and Macron, by the way, refuted that! He said the EU is disunited all by itself, and it's not China's fault.

So we have to see. Given the very close interweaving of the German and French economies and the specific history of the German-French relationship, one has to see how this plays out. Because I think that if Macron is taking such a leadership role at a moment when Germany does not have anything but a caretaker government, and Theresa May is very weakened because of the Brexit, then Macron has taken a leadership role for Europe. And I have the hope that the self-interest of German industry, the *Mittelstand*, where there is a growing interest, will eventually shift the policy. At the Sorbonne, the big university in Paris, they announced that they want to have 11 major conferences on the New Silk Road: The first one will be addressed by the former Prime Minister Dominique de Villepin.

So, I think the subject will be on the agenda and it will grow. Hopefully the Germans, who are resisting, as reflected in this very idiotic article in *FAZ*, will have to learn that if they don't want to be sidelined completely, they had better cooperate.

Schlanger: That brings us to the situation in the United States, where the President has continued to talk about the importance of the relationship with China, and yet, there seems to be a lot of pressure on him, from Wall Street, and from the so-called "deficit hawks" in Congress, to have no infrastructure plan in the United States.

Now, we did hear the other day that one of Trump's aides said that Trump is saying, "just spend the money." Where do things stand in terms of the United States' involvement with the potential promise of the Trump-Xi Jinping relationship?

Zepp-LaRouche: It's very difficult to say because part of the Republican Party is obviously not in favor of a credit system and Hamiltonian policies, which is the only way that you could finance such a massive infrastructure program. Trump said $1 trillion, the American Society of Civil Engineers talks about $4.5 trillion, and the Chinese even said what the United States really needs is $8 trillion. I would say that is a modest figure, given the fact that if you compare, China has now 22,000 km of high-speed rail systems; they want to have all major cities connected by high-speed rail by the year 2020, as compared to virtually no high-speed rail in the United States.

So there is no such system in the United States, and the bridges are falling apart, the subways are in bad shape, and then there is the damage from all of these hurricanes. So I think the only way that Trump could solve this problem is to fulfill one of his election promises to return to the American System of economy. That

means a national bank, and that means Glass-Steagall. And therefore, I think it's extremely good, Harley, that your article was just published on the website of Roger Stone, and I heard that six other websites also covered it. The headline of this article is, "Time Now for LaRouche's Economic Policies," and that is exactly to the point.

Our colleagues in the United States are distributing a new pamphlet, explaining why the United States should join the New Silk Road and implement the Four Laws of Lyndon LaRouche. Its title is, "LaRouche's Four Laws: The Physical Economic Principles for the Recovery of the United States—America's Future on the New Silk Road." And I would ask all the people who are watching this program to contact us and help us in the distribution of this pamphlet, and help shape what President Trump can do, because that is very largely a question of whether he has the support of his own constituency, against other interests, which want to prevent that. And obviously, if the Democrats were patriotic, they would just say, "Let's cooperate on Hamiltonian politics in an infrastructure buildup for the benefit of the country."

But I think it requires a major mobilization because of the forces who want to prevent it. You know, the people who think you need profit rates of 25%—which you don't get from infrastructure—who want to block this kind of investment, so it's a battle. And you listeners should join it in the right way.

Don't Pay Cash for Trash

Schlanger: I think the viewers should know, on the two major issues facing the United States, and facing the world right now, you and your husband have been at the forefront of putting forward the solutions: We've mentioned the work that you've done on the New Silk Road and publicizing the spirit of the New Silk Road.

We also have taken responsibility for fighting against the coup in the United States against Donald Trump. There were some developments on that in the

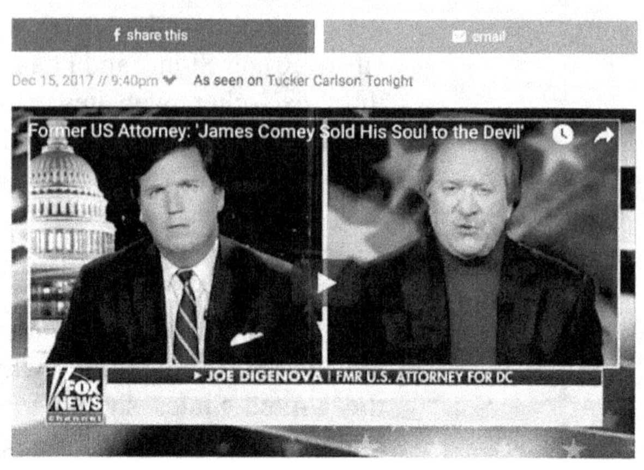

Fox News anchor Tucker Carlson (left) interviewing former U.S. Attorney for the District of Colombia, Joe DiGenova (right).

last couple of days, and we see the desperation of the anti-Trumpers, with this *Fire and Fury* book, and the calls for the 25th Amendment, attempting to say President Trump is childish or crazy or a danger. You also see Mueller threatening to interview Trump.

On the other side, our dossier on Mueller is getting very wide circulation, and this week there was a very strong statement from the former U.S. Attorney for Washington, D.C., Joseph DiGenova. That's quite a significant development, isn't it?

Zepp-LaRouche: It was on the largest radio station during morning drive-time in Washington, where Mr. DiGenova said that the people trying to oust Trump with this coup, that they're committing treason, and that he is certain that a criminal prosecution of all of those involved will follow. And then he went through all of their crimes, and he named all the names. This is not out of this world, because right now in the Congress, in the House Intelligence Committee, and in the Judiciary Committee in the Senate, the investigation is progressing. And I just heard that all the requested documents which [House Intelligence Chairman] Congressman Nunes had subpoenaed, have been delivered now. This pertains to the emails between Peter Strzok and Lisa Page; it pertains to the bank accounts of Fusion GPS, and similar documents.

So one can expect that light will be shed on all of this, and if things are really pursued, this could indeed lead to criminal prosecution with quite interesting results.

I think a sign of this new counteroffensive is also that President Trump's lawyer has now sued the very publication which went public with this terrible dossier of Christopher Steele. In the first place, this was *BuzzFeed* and also Fusion GPS. These suits are now launched, and it will get very interesting, because it's not decided. And this book *Fire and Fury* is such a lie-filled piece of trash-for-cash—people who buy this book should know that they're paying cash for trash.

So I think the situation is wide open, but it's not yet settled: It's a huge fight, and the role of the British, not only in the person of Christopher Steele, but also in the whole involvement of British intelligence in the coup against President Trump—has to come onto the table. Because it is not just evidence of treason in the United States, it's also what we call the British empire, which is the system which is situated with its headquarters in London. And it's about to go bankrupt, because we are looking at a new potential crash much worse than 2008.

All of this is very, very dramatic. But it's not hopeless, not at all.

Strike with Optimism

Schlanger: What's interesting is that you also see the defensiveness of the other side: Simpson, one of the founders of Fusion GPS, had an op-ed in the *New York Times*, and then the *BuzzFeed* editor also defended his position in producing this report and circulating it.

So I think there's a lot that can be said on this, but then on the other side, very interesting: With all the talk of the danger of President Trump—his infantile side and so on—you have the President of South Korea making a very strong statement, thanking President Trump for the openings between North and South. Where is that headed, Helga?

Zepp-LaRouche: That is very interesting, indeed. Because, on the 9th, two days ago, there was a meeting between the head of the unification committee of North Korea and the Unification Minister of South Korea, and they decided that North Korea will participate in the Olympic Games next month in South Korea; that the two delegations will march together as one into the Olympic Games; and that the Red Cross will help families to meet, which are divided between North and South.

Kim Jong-un said he would be willing to enter direct talks with the South Korean President. And as you mentioned, President Moon Jae-in said that Trump deserves a lot of credit, because it was Trump's policy which made all of this possible.

Now, as far as I know, this was not reported *anywhere* in the Western media! Even so, people should be very happy that in this very dangerous conflict around the Korea Peninsula, there are now signs that it can be overcome. And as we know, there were a lot of back-channel discussions between the United States and North Korea, and Russia and China and North Korea. Trump, Putin, and Xi were also on the telephone on these matters. So I think this is indeed something which goes to the credit of Trump, and the fact that the same media which are lying about him every five seconds, are not reporting that President Moon is thanking him, just shows how biased they are and that they are not concerned about the well-being of the people—neither those of North or South Korea, nor the rest of the world either.

But I think this is a very, very positive development, in a very dangerous world. And we should be optimistic that conflicts *can* be solved, through dialogue, through political means, and economic development; and the Korean situation is one very good example of that.

Schlanger: And just another point to emphasize that: The media are trying to get rid of Secretary of State Tillerson, saying that Trump is about to fire Tillerson; when Tillerson has openly said that U.S. policy is *not* regime change in North Korea, and I think that's played a role. And the *Wall Street Journal* just two days ago had an article saying the U.S. is game-planning for war in North Korea—should it be a small war, a limited nuclear war, and so on. And Defense Secretary Mattis came out and said we're not preparing for war, we prefer diplomacy.

So again, you have the lying media on the one side, and you have the actions in the world on the other.

Just to come back to what we started with, the developments around the New Silk Road, there has been a whole series of these—in Panama, Africa including Zimbabwe—and again, these are not being reported. I

Xinhua/Newsis

Representatives of the Democratic People's Republic of Korea (DPRK) and South Korea met Jan. 9, 2018 at the truce village of Panmunjom, and have agreed at the just-ended inter-Korean dialogue to hold separate military talks, with the DPRK also consenting to send a delegation to the 2018 Winter Olympics.

think it would be very useful if you could just give people a sense of how this is proceeding, including in the United States.

Role of France, Japan, the U.S.

Zepp-LaRouche: Well, you know, we published this book in 2014, *The New Silk Road Becomes the World Land-Bridge*, and that is what is happening. Because as the New Silk Road Spirit is catching on in many countries, we see now an agenda full of conferences on projects, and development proposals which were on the drawing boards for decades, but now they've become real. One big conference, for example, takes place at the beginning of February in Phuket, Thailand, cosponsored by the Chambers of Commerce of the British, French, Germans, and Australians in Thailand, on the Kra Canal. There's also high-level Japanese and Chinese involvement.

The Kra Canal would have *huge* significance for all of the ASEAN countries, because it would create a new sea route through Thailand. We had a conference on this in 1984 which was addressed by my husband. And this is obviously one of the big mega-projects. It would involve something like $55 billion, and it would be a tremendous economic stimulus for all of ASEAN, actually.

Then you have the very important development in Latin America, where Panama, which used to have diplomatic ties with Taiwan, shifted now to the one-China policy. There was a major state visit of the Panamanian President to China, and China is now building a major high-speed railroad from Panama City to a little town called David, at the border of Costa Rica. This has a signal effect for all the other Caribbean and Latin American countries that still have ties with Taiwan, because there is also tremendous cooperation of Chile with the New Silk Road. China is building a high-speed rail system there as well. And even in Brazil, support is growing for a bi-oceanic railroad from Brazil to Peru and also to other Latin American countries.

Also very important—I keep repeating this, because I think it's one of the key elements of strategic realignment in the world—is the fact that Prime Minister Abe of Japan has announced that he wants to put the relations between China and Japan on a new level; he wants to cooperate with the AIIB, the Asian Infrastructure Investment Bank; and he asked China if they could cooperate on projects in Africa together.

I think this is *really* significant, because if such conflicts as the one between China and Japan can be overcome through joint economic development in the New Silk Road, I think that is a sign of the future, and a sign of the "community of destiny" of which Xi Jinping talks, becoming a reality.

Additionally, the railroad between Djibouti and Addis Ababa has now officially opened, and there is a tremendous change of attitude! If you talk to Africans these days—diplomats or other people—they have a completely new self-confidence. They demand economic development, being treated as equal partners, and they don't want just to get sermons about human rights and democracy, and no development—which has been the attitude of the West so far.

So Macron is now making concrete plans—because after all, half of Africa is francophone, and France has an enormous expertise, in part for bad reasons, namely French colonialism, which in part was very bad. But the fact that Macron explicitly said that France does not want to repeat these mistakes, and therefore wants Chinese help through collaboration in Africa—I think this is incredible! And I wish that all African Americans in the United States would catch up with that and get engaged, because obviously, the United States could also play a very positive role if it were to cooperate in such economic development.

No Excuses!

There are some people who say this will never happen because the military-industrial complex in the United States will prevent it. But as my husband already pointed out in 2005 around the crisis of the U.S. auto industry, everything can be retooled! You can retool the plants you are using for military production to become part of a tremendous development program. That is a thought which will probably sound unlikely to some people, but I think that is the way to go! The question is, how can we build a world where we as humanity can survive and create really human conditions?

There are traditions in the United States associated with Lincoln, John Quincy Adams, Franklin D. Roosevelt, Kennedy; there are periods the United States could reconnect with, and then reach out and join hands with other nations such as China and Japan, in any case, but also Europeans, if they change. We should not be pessimistic and say these things cannot be changed.

I have found people who, as soon as you say these things, come up and say, "Oh, Macron is controlled by the bankers, so he will never do this," or, "He's not speaking the truth." Whatever you say, they have an answer, and they say, "This can never work." but I have found that many times this sort of pessimism is just a comfort zone, because once people have dug in their heels in their pessimism, it also means they don't have to do anything, because the world is hopeless in any case, so therefore you don't have to change it.

My attitude is, when things are developing in a positive direction, everybody—almost everybody on this planet—has the possibility for improvement and change for the better if the option is created. So therefore, I would appeal to people to have the culturally optimistic view on these matters, because to sit on your hands and do nothing at a moment of history like this one, is almost a crime.

Schlanger: Helga, the report you just gave makes the point that you and your husband have always made, which is that ideas are the most powerful force in shaping history, and too often, the people who submit to pessimism turn off their brains before they start speaking and saying those things. So I think people should take to heart what you just reported, go to our websites, look at the videos we're producing, download the dossiers, purchase the reports—the reports on West Asia and African development—and we can make this happen!

So with that, I think we'll conclude the webcast. Helga, thank you very much, and we'll see you next week.

Zepp-LaRouche: Yes, till next week.

Macron Promises European Cooperation with the New Silk Road!

by Helga Zepp-LaRouche, Chairwoman of the German Political Party
Bürgerrechtsbewegung Solidarität, BüSo, or Civil Rights Movement Solidarity

This article was written for Neue Solidarität and has been translated from German.

Jan. 12—The three-day state visit of French President Macron to China from January 8 to 10 marks a strategic breakthrough. In a one hour and 15 minute, very emotional and comprehensive speech in Xi'an, he announced France's solid cooperation with China's New Silk Road project, and pledged that he would be a reliable dialogue partner for China, committed to seeing all of Europe cooperate with this initiative. Not only has this started a new era for the relationship between China and France, as the Chinese media commented, but it has clearly highlighted France's role on the world stage.

The speech contained a whole series of features showing that Macron is responding to the new paradigm put on the strategic agenda by China's President Xi Jinping, with his idea of "win-win" cooperation among all nations—ideas that we would gladly hear from Berlin. The West must overcome the "unilateral imperialism" that France and other Western powers have pursued in Africa and elsewhere, he went on. "We have to learn the lessons of the past. Every time we tried to enforce the 'truth' or the 'law' against other peoples, we were wrong, and sometimes we even created an even worse situation. As in Iraq or in Libya today. We must work together to develop respect for the sovereignty of peoples." Macron condemned the West's claim of hegemony; our task is not the art of war, he said, but the art of cooperation in order to give the world the necessary harmony. He thanked China for creating, with the New Silk Road, a new epic, something which the "weary, post-modern" West is incapable of doing, because great epics are forbidden.

For the site of his speech, Macron had chosen Xi'an, a city rich in symbolism: both the Chinese starting point for the ancient Silk Road, and the birthplace of Xi Jinping. Macron clearly expressed his admiration for China's many contributions to the cultural history of humanity; to this day, he said, China is a land of inventors and engineers, always inventing the future. In Africa, where it has invested so much in infrastructure in recent years, he called on China to work with France and initiate joint projects that would be beneficial to the growth of the entire continent. The New Silk Road and a partnership between France and China, he went on, could help us avoid repeating France's old mistakes of "unilateral imperialism" in Africa.

Le Monde also struck an entirely new tone in republishing an article of the former chief economist of the

Xinhua

Presidents Emmanuel Macron (left) and Xi Jinping.

IMF, Simon Johnson, pointing to China's role as soon-to-be world leader in the field of innovation—a goal he considers already possible for this year. China has not only lifted 800 million people out of poverty within a short time, Johnson notes, it also built the world's largest high-speed rail system (22,000 km as of last year), and the annual consumption within China will rise to two trillion dollars by 2021, thus adding a consumer market the size of Germany to the world economy every year. Johnson is confident that by 2050 China will be the global powerhouse of scientific and technological innovation. (The article was first published in **Project Syndicate** at https:// www.project-syndicate.org/commentary/china-global-innovation-leader-by-simon-johnson-and-jonathan-ruane-2017-12.)

For his part, President Xi Jinping emphasized that he and Macron share the same views on many issues, and that both nations, as permanent members of the UN Security Council, have a special responsibility for peace and stability in the world.

Of strategic importance are extensive agreements for cooperation between the French nuclear corporation New Areva and the Chinese state-owned nuclear power company, China National Nuclear Corporation, as well as a space cooperation agreement. The two governments published a 27-point joint memorandum.

Two days after Macron's speech in Xi'an, the EU, which has hitherto been the main brake on Europe's cooperation with the New Silk Road, issued a memorandum of understanding, indicating that the EU now wants to come up with its own approach to building European connectivity, to be coordinated with the Chinese initiative. This was immediately welcomed by the Chinese Foreign Ministry.

And Germany?

Of all these developments, however, the citizens in Germany learn next to nothing. One day before Macron's speech in Xi'an, the *FAZ*'s Sunday edition printed a venomous tirade by one of its publishers, Holger Steltzner, titled "China's Road to World Power," which attempts to compete with the tone of the "Stürmer" or the "Schwar-

defenceimages.mod.uk

UK communications headquarters, GCHQ, British counterpart to the NSA.

zen Kanal." [Editor's note: these were propaganda organs of the Nazi movement and the East German government, respectively.] The author gives vent to his tantrum about "digital communists" with such abandon, that it is as if the GCHQ, NSA and Edward Snowden never existed. The purpose of the article, which picks up the "unilateral imperialism" of the West addressed by Macron and projects it upon China, is obviously to create paranoia among medium-sized companies that they may be taken over by communist cells. China is acting effectively against corruption, while plutocracy prevails unabashedly in the West, where despite triple-digit billion-dollar swindles, such as, for example, the LIBOR scandal, not a single banker has gone to jail. Also quoted is the head of MERICS (a think tank which supposedly knows all about China), Sebastian Heilmann, who warns of the "socialism with Chinese characteristics for a new era" and who should probably rename himself "disease man." [Editor's note: this is a joke on the name "Heilmann", which means "healing man."]

The problem with such tirades is not only that they are a malicious poisoning of the well, but that people in this country, in the absence of objective reporting on the most important strategic initiative not only for the world economy, but also for world peace, are being deprived of their right to be able to form their own opinion. It deprives them of the hope that there can actually be a positive future for humanity. What do you call that? Hope-icide?

All the more important, then, is Emmanuel Macron's intervention in China and his pledge to bring Europe into unified cooperation with the New Silk Road. The issue is now irrevocably on the table, regardless of the conceptual pitfalls that lie along the way.

The party leaders of Germany's Grand Coalition, however, who have just reached an agreement to form a government, have as yet not uttered a word about cooperation with the New Silk Road or about Macron's pledge. Both Macron and the representatives of the planned Grand Coalition want to promote the further integration of Europe, with a banking union, a capital market union and the exchange and control of data. Beside the fact that

German voters will hardly be enthusiastic about seeing even more money flow into the opaque, unloved mega-bureaucracy in Brussels, what has been announced so far leaves the essential problems completely out of the picture.

The main reason that the southern European countries have been driven into ruin by the Troika's austerity policies, as well as why no infrastructure investments have been made—be it in the Balkans or in Germany—and why the countries of Eastern, Central and Southern Europe are so openly in favor of cooperation with China, has to do

European Central Bank headquarters.

with the "debt brake" and "black zero" policies (both concerned with balancing budgets), and the ECB policy in favor of speculators. The continuation of these policies after 2008 means that we are facing a much bigger crash than at that time. If the EU and the potential new German Grand Coalition stick to this policy, the new EU plan will be just as impossible to implement as the famous Juncker plan, whose financing amounted to the proverbial "peanuts."

Nothing less will do than the realization of the Four Laws, which Lyndon LaRouche has defined as an absolute prerequisite for overcoming the crisis: a Glass-Steagall banking separation system, a new credit System in the tradition of Alexander Hamilton, and full integration into the principles of the New Silk Road, which Xi Jinping calls a "community of destiny for mankind." What China is presenting are really radically new ideas in strategic terms, and people in Europe should not be so arrogant as to dismiss it or see it as a threat.

These ideas of Xi Jinping, however, are in principle very much in line with the principles of the humanist tradition of Europe, in the sense that they place the common good and the creativity of man at the center of politics. In addition, we need a political discourse that does not exist at all in the oh-so-democratic West, but certainly does in China.

zepp-larouche@eir.de

May 29, 2009

Economy For Scientists: Economic Science, In Short

by Lyndon H. LaRouche, Jr.

The following report has been produced for the special benefit of those serious scientists and poets who are prepared to come directly to the crucial issue underlying the world's presently accelerating plunge into the onrushing new dark age of general breakdown-crisis of the present world economy as a whole. The subject within which this report is situated, is what is, to my present knowledge, the still rarely considered principle which distinguishes the human mind, knowledgeably, from that of beasts. This is the same uniquely human principle, of that willful potential of the human mind which lies under the same heading, under which the notion of the ontological conception of the tensor must be situated for our study here.

Foreword

Unless there is a relatively immediate reversal of the current economic and demographic policies which had been expressed by both the recent U.S. Presidency of George W. Bush, Jr., and, now, President Barack Obama, civilization on this planet is now doomed to a rapidly accelerating descent of all mankind in a general dark age, a time during which the population of this planet would descend, foreseeably, from the presently estimated level of more than six-and-a-half billions persons, to the less than two billions which has been the stated goal of Britain's Prince Philip and the Prince's explicitly pro-genocidal World Wildlife Fund.

This nightmare, born out of current British ideology, which is already now descending upon this planet as a whole, is not a product of natural causes, but, rather, the natural outcome of so-called Malthusian economic policies, policies which had been radiated from the British empire, and had been carried out, during a certain time, by what the British monarchy and its ideological accomplices and interests had created as the Nazi Germany regime under Adolf Hitler, earlier. The same kind of genocidal result packaged as the Hitler regime, is being promoted by the British under the impetus of Prince Philip and his World Wildlife Fund now, with the present collaboration of U.S. President Barack Obama.

These pro-genocidal policies of the current British monarchy, are of a type which is by no means new to known history. The current policies of the British monarchy, of its accomplices inside leading political and related circles inside even our own United States, and its current Presidential administration today, are types of policies which the Eighteenth-Century British Empire's British East India Company of Lord Shelburne and his accomplices had copied, explicitly, from the policies of practice of the ancient Roman Empire, policies which had been described in the **Prometheus Bound** of the ancient Greek Classical dramatist Aeschylus.

The continuation of such pro-genocidal policies as those of Britain's Prince Philip and his World Wildlife Fund today, is not to be traced to the United Kingdom as a nation-state, but, rather, to the imperial character of the role of London's financial center as the capital of a world-wide empire based on a currently dominant world-wide monetarist system akin to a Keynesian monetarist system. This is a system whose origins are traced to the feudal medieval European monetarist system, centered in Venice, which crashed in the so-called "New Dark Age" of Europe's Fourteenth Century, and to the monetarist imperial system of usury maintained by the Roman and Byzantine empire earlier. That is the present-day echo of the imperialist form of tyranny, an echo which is known by the name of "globalization" today.

"Globalization" and the attempted global practice of genocide, by the British monarchy and its accomplices, against the world's population today, is a presently immediate threat to all mankind which has arisen in its present form through the virtual capture of the Presidency of the United States by the British monarchy, as under the recent and current Presidencies of George H.W. Bush (1989-1993), George W. Bush, Jr. (2001-2009), and, presently, Barack Obama (2009 -…).

President Obama and his immediate personal cabal of the pro-genocidal British fanatics gathered within his Presidency, is a present expression of the particular, greatest economic threat to mankind as a whole. It is an expression of the influence of the British monarchy's currently continuing tradition of Lord Shelburne's British East India Company, a tradition of hateful efforts against all mankind during the course of the modern world history since that February 1763 Peace of Paris which established that Company as, in fact of practice, a private world maritime empire holding the British monarchy itself as captive.

The United Kingdom, as a form of an only nominally sovereign nation-state, had become, up to the present time, a virtual colony of what Shelburne established, in 1782, as the British Foreign Office and its relationship to a City of London as a center of a global form of imperial monetarist system. President Obama, like the present regime of the U.S. Federal Reserve System, is presently a collateral puppet of that continuing, global form of monetarist imperium crafted according to the paradigm of the Roman, Byzantine, and Venetian traditions.

The mission of Columbus, to find, across the Atlantic, a place to secure a future for what was then an imperilled European civilization—what was to become our United States—was the outgrowth of the influence of Cardinal Nicholas Cusa (above).

Our United States

It is an, unfortunately, little known, but crucial fact of all modern world history, that what was to become our United States, was the outgrowth of the influence of the then-deceased Cardinal Nicholas Cusa, since about A.D. 1480, in motivating Captain Christopher Columbus to take a known passage across the Atlantic Ocean, a voyage intended to find, on a newly rediscovered continent, a place from which to secure a new future for that, then imperilled, new European civilization which had been launched by the great ecumenical Council of Florence.

It was that mission, adopted by Columbus, which set into motion what was to become our United States. Such was, also, the expressed intention of the mission which launched the Pilgrim and Massachusetts Bay settlements in what became known as New England. These settlers were not refugees, but true pioneers embarked upon a mission to give birth to new hope for a European civilization which was being torn apart, in Europe itself, by the monstrous evils of the prolonged religious warfare of 1492-1648. The intention of these trans-Atlantic settlements, was to create a new world system of sovereign nation-state republics, as had been proposed by Nicholas of Cusa's **Concordancia Catholica** (establishing the modern nation-state), his **De Docta Ignorantia** (the founding of modern European science), and his **De Pace Fidei** (his ecumenical policy).

There were similar attempts launched across the Atlantic from Spain, but it came to be the English-speaking settlements in North America which produced the unique form of self-government, later emulated by notable cases of Spanish speaking nations there, as expressed, most notably, by those who reacted against the imperial intentions of the British East India Company's attempted tyranny, in 1763.

The British East India Company went on, to become a world empire, absorbing the British monarchy itself by, cleverly, like an infectious disease, being swallowed by it. Through wars which Anglo-Dutch Liberal agents of the new European imperial party either launched, or provoked, beginning that so-called "Seven Years War" celebrated by the East India Company's February 1763 Peace of Paris, and through such successors of the same divide-and-rule warfare, as the Napoleonic wars, what became World Wars I and II, and also "The Cold War," that British Empire worked to secure the ruin of those nation states whose independence would be a threat to the British imperial monetarists' design for their intended world maritime empire.

The essence of this Anglo-Dutch, imperial monetarist scheme, commonly known as the British Empire, has always been an extended expression of the monetarist systems typified by the issues of: the Peloponnesian War; the wars of the Roman and Byzantine empires; the Venetian model of imperial monetarism associated with European feudalism; and, despite important periodic resistance to this, most of modern European practice.

In short, *monetarism is the essence of a specifically European imperialism* extant, as a kind of infectious disease, since the Peloponnesian War. The essence of such empires has been the existence of a privately held, monopolistic system of credit, in the form of a monetary system. It is a system which remains opposed to a truly sovereign, national credit-system in the likeness of what the U.S. Federal Constitution prescribed as a "Hamiltonian" national banking policy for our Federal republic. That policy of our republic, has always been, as under the leadership of our President Franklin D. Roosevelt, and President Abraham Lincoln before him, the greatest threat to imperialism ever existing in modern world history to date.

In short, the British empire hates us, but admires the

A 'Hamiltonian' National Banking Policy for the U.S.

Here are excerpts from the U.S. Constitution, Article I Section 8, which, as LaRouche writes, represents "a truly sovereign, national credit-system," that is, "a 'Hamiltonian' national banking policy for our Federal republic."

The Congress shall have power to lay and collect taxes, duties, imposts and excises, to pay the debts and provide for the common defense and general welfare of the United States; but all duties, imposts and excises shall be uniform throughout the United States;

To borrow money on the credit of the United States;

To regulate commerce with foreign nations, and among the several states, and with the Indian tribes;

To establish a uniform rule of naturalization, and uniform laws on the subject of bankruptcies throughout the United States;

To coin money, regulate the value thereof, and of foreign coin, and fix the standard of weights and measures;

To provide for the punishment of counterfeiting the securities and current coin of the United States;

To establish post offices and post roads;

To promote the progress of science and useful arts, by securing for limited times to authors and inventors the exclusive right to their respective writings and discoveries;

…—And

To make all laws which shall be necessary and proper for carrying into execution the foregoing powers, and all other powers vested by this Constitution in the government of the United States, or in any department or officer thereof.

---

breeding and promotions of the parasites and ruinously degrading immoralities it has bred within our economy and customs.

'I Am a Paradigmatic Patriot!'

Clearly, the Obama Presidency must be either soon reformed, to purge it of its complicity in such implicitly treasonous policies as those practiced by both the George W. Bush administration and the Obama administration itself, since September 2007; or, in the alternative, it must be replaced by means of constitutional due process now. President Obama has virtually no secure choice but that. Either he reverses his present policies, especially his rabidly unconstitutional, Hitler-like, healthcare policies, or it will be either him or the United States as a nation, or both, which will be destroyed very soon. World history has already had one attempt, by Adolf Hitler, at such an imperial regime, and civilization will not readily tolerate another such epidemic.

In short, history would not tolerate a new, would-be "Emperor Nero" for long.

It is a good, but perilous endeavor to be a patriot in our present "time that tries men's souls." It is also urgent that our remedies be competent ones. Since the root for the cure of our society's onrushing catastrophe, lies in the need for a competent economic policy, my own patriotic contribution is unique. In fact, as fairly competent economists will come to recognize, our nation's life depends upon adoption of what I have to say here and now. I am, in that way, a paradigmatic patriot.

Therefore, herewith, in the following body of this report, I shall proceed as follows. I shall begin with the introduction of some indispensable essentials of economics practiced as a science. I point out the commonplace errors of opinion about economy, opinion of which we must rid the governing circles of our nation, if this nation is actually to survive.

The most profound and widespread failure presently pervading most scientific thought, including a science of economy, as taught and believed today, is expressed as what I identify here as the pathological quality of the presumptions of the so-called "Anglo-

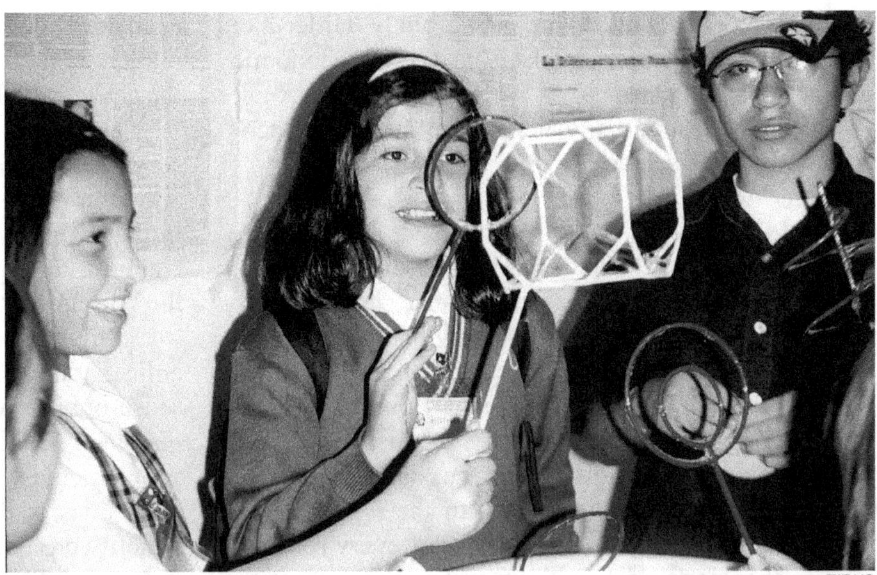

EIRNS

The child's primary experience of the universe is not a direct representation of the actual universe; although it does have the means to bring about changes in that world, and, by means of those changes, the mind gains access to knowledge of the world out there, beyond mere sense-perceptions. Here, children in Lima, Peru experience the shadows of the real universe, in a music and geometry workshop, 2004.

Dutch empiricists." Their first error is their presumption, that sense-perception provides us a direct insight into what we should consider, if not as the real universe, but, nonetheless, what they regard as if it were the real universe; for them, the rest is "merely theory." The second is the associated presumptions, such as those inherently corrupting, *a-priori* definitions, axioms, and postulates of Euclidean geometry, which were overthrown categorically by Bernhard Riemann's 1854 habilitation dissertation.

So, the modern empiricists, such as the followers of Adam Smith, insist, still to the present day, that there is no existence of truth, but, instead, only customary, implicitly statistical, or kindred presumptions, presumptions which are premised, in turn, upon more or less blind obedience to mere sense-perceptions.[1] That denial of the existence of any truth, is the underlying premise of the entire doctrine of President Obama's currently

---

1. The tragic incompetence, exhibited in its effects by the presently onrushing global economic breakdown-crisis, is typical of virtually all modern economists of today's Anglo-Dutch Liberal school. See Adam Smith, **Theory of Moral Sentiments** (1759). The fascist bio-ethical policies of President Obama are based almost entirely on this work of Adam Smith. Cf. Lyndon H. LaRouche, Jr., et al., **The Ugly Truth About Milton Friedman** (New York: New Benjamin Franklin House, 1980).

stated, radically Malthusian, and frankly Hitler-like health-care policies, and, also, his related economic policies generally.

This now brings us to the crucial matters of economics as a true science.

What Is Science?

Contrary to such delusions as those of President Obama currently, the truth is, that human sense-perceptions are fairly described as: "merely instrument readings," rather than being "a direct sense of the real universe as such." Those "instrument readings," at least some among the entire roster, remain indispensable for us; but, they are clear to us only on the condition, that we recognize the fact, that, contrary to the *a-priori* presumptions of Euclid, from the outset of every relevant inquiry, that instrument readings, such as those of sense-perception, or otherwise, are just that, rather than being "self-evident" ideas of nature in and of themselves.

The tendency of those persons who are ignorant of this distinction, has been to believe in sense-certainty, more or less as the empiricist followers of Paolo Sarpi have defined it. That latter, empiricist, tendency, as radiated by the global influence of what is called "The British Empire" of today, is, in fact, the source of the greatest single moral crisis, as much as an intellectual crisis, among the cultures of the world presently.

Contrary to such pathological tendencies, the power of the human mind to know reality, lies actually within that mind as such; the senses, like all, either inborn, or man-made instrumentation used by us to explore our experience, present the creative powers of the human mind with the "data" which serves as the challenge posed by the fact, that it is from the human mind's apprehension of the *subsuming dynamics* of those relationships, among those mere shadows, from which we adduce that experimental evidence, from which, in turn, that mind must adduce the functional existence of what is to be recognized as the efficient reality among mental objects.[2]

Those subsuming *dynamics* are expressed as demonstrable universal physical principles, as that point is illustrated by Johannes Kepler's uniquely original discovery of the universal principle of gravitation in the Solar system. These are real objects whose sensed presence is adumbrated by those "shadows" which, when cast, are to be recognized as merely "shadows" cast by reality, as merely sense-perceptions, not the reality of the action which those shadows reflect.[3]

Thus, the human mind, as such, has no directly sensory access to the reality of the world which it inhabits: although it does have the means to bring about changes in that world, and, it is by exactly the means of those changes, that that mind gains access to knowledge of the "world out there, beyond mere sense-perceptions."

At first glance, we might, admittedly, think, mistakenly, that the mind's experience is limited to the role of sense-organs, which are merely a source of instrument readings. This means either inborn sense-organs, or supplementary, man-made instruments which serve as extensions of those functions of those built-in senses, which were delivered with "the package" which was the new child. Thus, that child's primary experience of the universe which mankind inhabits, is not a direct representation of the actual universe which we inhabit; but, rather, it is a kind of shadow cast on the mind, which is expressed, cumulatively, as a *dynamic* pattern among shadows; it is that, subsuming, *dynamic* pattern, in the sense of the *dynamis* of the ancient Pythagoreans and Plato, or the *dynamics* of Gottfried Leibniz, from which we are to adduce that higher principle, such as the universal gravitation discovered, uniquely, by Johannes Kepler, as in his **The Harmonies of the World**, which has cast such patterns among shadows.

It is from the subsuming, *dynamic* relations manifest in the process of man's practice upon the patterns of the "instrument readings," that we are able to adduce the real universe which casts those shadows which we experience as sense-perceptions. This was the fact emphasized by Gottfried Leibniz during the 1690s, in his exposure of the scientifically fraudulent character of the presumptions on which not only the system of Rene Descartes depended, but also those Anglo-Dutch Eighteenth-century empiricists who attacked the very memory of Leibniz's existence, fraudulently, on this account, after he was dead: such lying hoaxsters were the hoaxsters de Moivre, D'Alembert, Leonhard Euler, Joseph Lagrange, and also Laplace and the plagiarist swindler Augustin Cauchy.[4]

---

2. I.e., the ancient Pythagoreans' *dynamis*, and the modern *dynamics* of Gottfried Leibniz.

3. For example, there was never any truth in the allegation that Isaac Newton discovered gravitation. All arguments which insist that Newton discovered gravitation are nothing but outright frauds.

4. As I have made the same point in earlier locations, this notion of dynamics also appears implicitly in the concluding paragraph of Percy Bysshe Shelley's **A Defence of Poetry**.

It is through experience, that the human foetus and infant begin to assemble what becomes a sense of the notion of that individual's relationship to those sense-experiences as such. So, the development of the foetus, infant, and child, is not experienced as a replica of the universe it might be thought to be merely experiencing in this way; it is a reflection of that experience of our sense of those changes which we are able to effect within the universe itself, as, within our own patterns of behavior. It is through the newly emerging individual, in this way, that the mind of the emerging child comes to recognize its interaction, through the senses, among individual creatures whose actually *dynamic* patterns of response have what becomes recognized as a specific quality of kinship with that child's own nature.[5]

Among the results which may emerge in the continuation of this process, the following notable cases are to be included.

Within the bounds of a modern, Twentieth-century and Twenty-First-century physical science, the matter of that distinction is to be located now, most directly, and most efficiently, as at the center of the interacting deliberations of Albert Einstein and Academician V.I. Vernadsky on the subject of what is called the *tensor*, as expressing a physical conception, rather than merely a mathematical one. *Dynamics* (or, the ancient *dynamis*) are synonymous with the concept of the *tensor*, when this matter is considered as a subject and product of the method of Bernhard Riemann. As Leibniz attacked Descartes explicitly on this point, the *dynamic* (e.g., *tensor*) is the proper subject of science; the sensory or like forms of experience are the products (predicates) of that subject.[6]

On this account, great minds, such as Bernhard Riemann and such among his most relevant followers, as Albert Einstein and Academician Vernadsky, appear to us today as having been what are called "true geniuses," chiefly, because they had reached the stage of moral and intellectual maturity at which they are not to be mistaken for populist-like dupes of blind faith in sense-certainty as such. They are, rather, focused, less on events as such, than on processes of changes; they think so in the sense of Leibniz's introduction of the modern term *dynamics,* with emphasis on those kinds of changes manifestly induced and controlled by relevant kinds of willful actions by the human mind itself.[7]

The Principle of Economy

On this account, all that is contrary to what I report here, but which is generally taught and believed teachings in the name of "economics" today, is to be thrown into the waste-paper basket. Not carelessly, as if all at once, not arbitrarily, but through a process of distinguishing, step by step, experimentally, actual from merely presumed knowledge. So, for example, once reigning superstitions in the form of viciously reductionist fallacies of composition respecting economy, are put aside in this way.

However, in the meantime, there is already no remaining basis for the widespread, but delusionary belief, that some intrinsic value is expressed by money. Value is expressed, not as a quantity *per se*, but only as *the relative effects of the increase, or decrease of the physical potential relative population-density of the individual in society*. The value of money lies not in the individual exchange, but in the functional unity (*unifying dynamic*) of the social process of a nation, or nations when considered as an individual, *dynamic* entirety.[8]

On a deeper, far more important level than that, the issue to be considered is, that, essentially, the individual person must become capable of seeing each among themselves in his, or her society, as expressing the mind which makes use of the mere instrument-readings we call sense-perceptions, rather than, mistakenly, locating the person himself, or herself, as like a creature belonging, ontologically, to the illusory domain of that shadow-world called "sense-certainty." This is an ex-

---

5. E.g., Gottfried Leibniz, "Critical Thoughts on the General Part of the Principles of Descartes" (1692). See also, Leibniz, **Specimen Dynamicum** (1695). In **Gottfried Wilhelm Leibniz: Philosophical Papers and Letters**, Leroy E. Loemker, ed. (Boston: Kluwer Academic Publishers, 1989).

6. Ibid.

7. So, Kepler's uniquely original discovery of a principle of universal gravitation, as detailed in his **The Harmonies of the World**, defined a principle of universal gravitation as if bounding the action within the ordering of the Solar system, rather than a kinematic interaction among those bodies. Albert Einstein, in reviewing this discovery by Kepler as implicitly Riemannian, defined the universe as "finite, but unbounded."

8. On this account, all British economists, such as Adam Smith, Jeremy Bentham, and their followers, have based the entirety of their dogmas on utter frauds. The fascist types of so-called economists, such as the charlatans associated with the policy-making of President Barack Obama, are examples of what tends to become the mass-murderous character of such frauds. Hence, in the latter cases: mass-murderously criminal frauds.

pression of that principle of *dynamics* on which all competent practice of a science of economy depends, any competent notion of "economic value," most emphatically.

What tends the most to conceal the true nature of the human individual from himself, or herself, is the tendency for belief in sense-certainty, as that pathological disordering of the human mind, is typified by the a-priori *presumptions of Euclidean geometry, and, similarly, the grave error, as this was pointed out by Philo of Alexandria, as the error of presuming, that the Creator of the universe had lost the power of creativity, once an initial Creation had occurred. It is only to the degree, that the individual recognizes that the reality of his, or her existence, does not lie in the mere shadows of what are often, mistakenly, supposed sense-certainty, as such, that the individual rises to an efficiently conscious awareness of the reality of one's own functioning, a reality which lies within the individual's historical identity within the historical-cultural process of society as a whole.*

It is here, beyond vulgar, populist's, or kindred sorts of erroneous notions of space and time, that true scientific reality, as known presently to only the greatest poets, musicians, and scientists, reposes in that which is often misnamed by the confused in their misuse of the term "spiritual" domain.

So, Percy Bysshe Shelley wrote in the concluding paragraph of his 1819 **A Defence of Poetry**. There, in that place, in a passage which is usually misunderstood still today, he points toward the only place where the presence of the access to immortality of the individual human soul can be found, in that domain of *an eternal simultaneity of human immortality*, under which mankind's proper conception of space and time reposes.

It is in the unity of science and Classical poetry (and polyphony), that the efficient unity of experience of physical practice and creativity (Classical artistic composition) are unified as a single process.

In that true domain of human individual existence, time, like space, is merely another sensory experience to be made knowable to us through the powers specific to human individual creativity. It is real only in the sense that time and space are known as being, efficiently, an adumbration of reality for us, rather than being, as for the dupes of Descartes, each some independent faculty outside and above the actual physical domain.

Art, Science & Creativity

Since, most emphatically, the discoveries by Johann Sebastian Bach, the most alert minds of science and music alike, have recognized that poetic principle of what is called Classical musical composition, as the experience of the unity of effect of mind, matter, space and time. So, matters were considered by the relevant greatest minds of the time prior to the 1890-1989 period of general threat of "world war" throughout our planet. Thus, prior to the recent rise of the so-called "modernist" hostility against the legacy of Bach, a hostility had come on, like a new bubonic plague of the soul: so, now, as during the preceding Twentieth Century, in the worsening state of mind and morals already prevalent, now, in the first decade of the Twenty-First, we have come to live in four or more recent decades during which there has been an accumulated loss of that connection to the Classical revolution in both science and Classical music, painting, and poetry, a connection on which the greatest achievements of modern European civilization had depended during the immediately preceding centuries.

Within certain limits, we can, and must say, that the modern world history, since the accession of the novel, Anglo-Dutch Liberal form of British monarchy of England's George I, but, most emphatically, since the February 1763 Peace of Paris, has been a period of a special quality of wars and other great struggles between good and evil, a war, on the one side, which had achieved what was typified by the founding of our United States as a constitutional republic, and, on the opposing side, the intrinsic evil of British imperialism, the latter an evil which presently dominates the world, now including the United States, through British, Venetian-style shaping of the present world's monetarist system, today. That has not been essentially a conflict between nations, but a conflict of two fundamentally different principles of two opposing world systems: two mutually exclusive conceptions of the nature of mankind.

Any contrary view of that period of modern history is fairly described as being, at its best, politically and scientifically childish, *and actually bestial.*

It is to be said, without any justified fear that we might be exaggerating, that there has been a generally accelerating moral decay in U.S. culture since the April 12, 1945 death of President Franklin Roosevelt. The process of moral decay in the U.S.A. since the April 13, 1945 inauguration of President Harry S Truman, was

"Since, most emphatically, the discoveries by Johann Sebastian Bach, the most alert minds of science and music alike, have recognized that poetic principle of what is called Classical musical composition, as the experience of the unity of effect of mind, matter, space, and time." Left: J.S. Bach (painting by Elias Gottlob Haussmann, 1748); right: LaRouche Youth Movement chorus performs Bach's "Jesu, meine Freude," November 2006.

accelerated in the immediate aftermath of the assassination of President John F. Kennedy; not long after that, came a steep decline into a new fascist wave of the late Spring 1968, fascist movement merely typified by the depravity of Mark Rudd and his associates. During the 1970s, the U.S. Nixon Administration was already a fascist administration in intent, as was the U.S. Carter Administration, to the degree it was under the control of the Trilateral Commission of David Rockefeller and Zbigniew Brzezinski.

This trend in depravity of civilization has been accelerated globally by the post-1989 actions of wrecking the sovereignties of the nations of continental Europe, by the trio of British Minister Margaret Thatcher, President George H.W. Bush, and French President François Mitterrand. This wrecking was accelerated later, as, later, by the frankly social-fascist, Fabian British Prime Minister Tony Blair, by U.S. President George W. Bush, Jr., and, now, the introduction of the 1939-1945 criminal, pro-genocide health-care practices of Adolf Hitler, under the U.S. Presidency of a fascist-controlled, corporatist administration introduced by President George W. Bush, Jr. and, since January 2007, by Speaker of the House Nancy Pelosi, as now accelerated, again, since the latter Bush Presidency, under Barack Obama, to the present moment these words are written.

Fascism & President Obama

Contrary to the silly, self-deluding opinions of some governments in Eurasia, unless the currently Hitler-tending, present policies of the Barack Obama administration are reversed, very soon, there will be the conclusive experience of a general, convulsive, chain-reaction form of breakdown-crisis of the economy of the entire planet, under the presently prevalent conditions and policies throughout the planet, especially trans-Atlantic policies now. Once the reality of that challenge is taken into account, another challenge confronts us, a positive, rather than a negative one.

There are various ways in which a description of that higher challenge might be approximated. From a practical standpoint, the immediate problem to be overcome, is the habituated incompetence of what is currently being experienced, world-wide, as the accepted practice of university teaching and nations' policy-shaping in the shaping of economic policies of current general practice. The point has now been reached, that unless and until that problem is corrected, there is no hope for a continuation of a civilized form of life on this planet, for a generation or more to come.

The Hitler-like variety of fascist ideology embedded as the expression of the Behaviorist ideology of President Barack Obama's current health-care doctrine, is located in that President's presently manifest lack of ability to distinguish human nature, functionally, from that of expendable members of colonies of baboons. His choice of a health-care policy which is an explicit copy of the death-camp-style of health-care ideology of the Nazi dictator Adolf Hitler, reflects that President's lack of any effective comprehension of the essential difference between beast and man.

Nowhere in the equation, has President Obama allowed space for a categorical quality of systemic distinction between people and cullable herds of cattle. On this account, his behavior, thus far, has not been fairly describable as human. Since the qualification for President of the U.S.A. is that the incumbent be human, not only in flesh, but in mind, he must now consider himself obliged to choose between continuing to be President, under a radically improved policy-forming matrix, or sent into retirement from public office, perhaps even to the political equivalent of a cattle-farm or a public zoo.

Presently, he has become a moral as well as an intellectual disaster. His behavior has turned his now fractured oath of office into a moral, and almost biological disaster. His ties to the British monarchy of the consummately evil Prince Philip of World Wildlife Fund bestiality, are therefore to be featured as among the first considerations in suggesting the causes to be taken into account, in defining the President's tendency for degeneracy, as thus shown at this juncture.

For this present case, not only merely the correction of President Obama's shocking recent misconduct, but also a deeper insight into the principles of a physical science of economy, is necessary. That challenge is our subject here.

I. The Science of Physical Economy

Before coming to the details of economic systems as social systems, we must first situate the principled quality of the *functionally physical characteristics of economies* within the notion of the essential relationship of the existence of the human species-type to that planet (and Solar system) which we inhabit.

In opening the following body of this report, thus, I must emphasize, once more, that science can not be competently premised upon a notion of sense-certainty. The real universe is not the so-called "materialist's"

world of sense-experience as such. Rather, as I have already emphasized here, earlier, our sense-experiences are merely shadows, like "meter-readings," of the reality which naive persons mistake for a "self-evident" universe. So, Johannes Kepler discovered the universal principle of gravitation, in his **The Harmonies of the World**, by rejecting naive belief in the allegedly self-evident, in favor of accepting the reality of the actually ironical juxtaposition, within the processes of the Solar system, of the sense of sight with respect to the sense of musical harmonies.

Listen to me patiently, as I outline the seemingly paradoxical case which we must consider here and now.

It is the paradoxical juxtaposition of contrasted dimensions of sense-experiences, which defines the object of the human intellect as such, and which supplies the intellectual solution for *the ostensibly paradoxical character of that real existence which casts those shadows called sense-perceptions*.

In terms of the formalities of modern thinking about science, the needed notion employed in this report, appeared in Nineteenth and Twentieth centuries' physical science with the presentation of the roots of the concept of the *tensor* in the work of Carl F. Gauss, as in his discovery of the orbit of the asteroid Ceres. This connection was made clearer by the 1854 habilitation dissertation of Bernhard Riemann, and, still later, as Gauss's and Riemann's successive contributions were extended into Twentieth-century scientific practice, through the successive work of Albert Einstein and Academician V.I. Vernadsky.

Throughout the history of the *tensor*, from its modern roots in the discoveries of Nicholas of Cusa's follower Johannes Kepler, through the relevant discoveries of Pierre de Fermat and the dynamics of Gottfried Leibniz, into the modern, Riemannian physics of Einstein and Vernadsky, the available and necessary viewpoint of a competent notion of political-economy, employs the combined effect of both the natural human senses and the supplementary "senses" of scientific instruments, to adduce the mind's grasp of the real object of experimental knowledge, adducing that from the behavior of that mere shadow cast by the combined means given to us by the intersections among both the natural and artificial senses. This requirement, which assumed shape through the discoveries of Riemann, has come to represent an expandable set of given and acquired synthetic sense-perceptions, which the device of the *tensor*

Karl Gauss   *Johannes Kepler*

Bernhard Riemann   *V. I. Vernadsky*

"Throughout the history of the tensor, from its modern roots in the discoveries of Nicholas of Cusa's follower Johannes Kepler, through the relevant discoveries of Fermat and the dynamics of Leibniz, into the modern, Riemannian physics of Einstein and Vernadsky, the available and necessary viewpoint of a competent notion of political-economy, employs the combined effect of both the natural human senses and the supplementary 'senses' of scientific instruments, to adduce the mind's grasp of the real object of experimental knowledge, adducing that from the behavior of that mere shadow cast by the combined means given to us by the intersections among both the natural and artificial senses."

permits us to construct, as a mentally synthesized image, used to supersede naive reliance on the phantoms of sense-certainty.

When we look back to, for example, to the legacy of the *Sphaerics* of the ancient Pythagoreans and Plato, and view those ancient physical sciences in modern Nineteenth and Twentieth centuries' terms, we are presently obliged to shift the teaching and practice of science, away from the image of the mere shadows of sensory certainties, to a mental image of the *tensor*, defined by the methods introduced through the impact of the successive contributions of Gauss and Riemann. It is

the latter, mental, image which frees the mind of the modern scientist from the phantoms of sense-certainty.

This presently obligatory viewpoint of that modern science, *when including the science of physical economy,* places the nature of man and society, finally, in its appropriate perspective.

That Actual Universe

Thus, the relevant point of reference needed for a clear understanding of the present challenge to the world's economists, is to be located within a relative coincidence, which can be found between Albert Einstein and Academician V.I. Vernadsky, on the concept of the *tensor*. In broad terms, both agreed. However, there is an important qualification posed by the refinement supplied by Vernadsky.

The crucial distinction between those two great scientists of our preceding century, is that between Einstein's approach to the notion of a physical universe as such, and Vernadsky's correction, we meet the image of Einstein's universe redefined by Vernadsky, as being composed actually of a dynamic interaction among the *abiotic*, the *Biosphere*, and the *Noösphere*. The form of the method of both of these authorities, is otherwise common; the results differ in the matter of the functional significance of certain subsumed issues of ontology.

The Biosphere expresses a principle of life, which is expressed only by processes which are specifically either living, or having come into existence, as being specifically *products of* the action of *a universal physical principle of life.*

The Noösphere expresses a principle of human creative powers *uniquely specific* to the system of living individual human beings. Human beings' biologically living bodies would be, if only apparently, a part of the Biosphere, except, that the behavior of no other living creature, has the characteristics of those specifically human creative powers, powers which distinguish the functional role of the human species, *human life,* as a species of existence, to be distinguished, absolutely, from, and above all other known forms of life.

Therefore, I have demanded that the standpoint of the *Noösphere* be chosen as the required standard for a competent practice of a science of physical economy, and, therefore, all policy-shaping in general. In all matters, the human species is to be distinguished as a cognitive species, primarily, that to such effect, that the person is defined primarily as a cognitive being with creative attributes absent in lower forms of life, and the living human organism is treated as a vehicle for expression of what is, essentially, the cognitive being.[9]

For purposes of illustrating the most crucial distinctions to be made here, I summarize the essential point to be made in the following terms of "fair approximation."

Whatever may have been the additions, or deductions, from the mass attributable to the planet Earth, the patterns of changes in the relative mass of the "Lithosphere," Biosphere, and Noösphere, are the following:

a.) The accumulated relative mass of products of the Biosphere, has been increased relative to the "Lithosphere."

b.) The relative mass of the Noösphere, has been increased relative to the Biosphere, and at a greater rate than for the Biosphere.

c.) The characteristic internal feature of change in the planet on these combined accounts, has been that quality of human creativity unique to the human individual mind, as attested by the anti-reductionists' creativity of our greatest scientists and Classical poets.

d.) *The creative powers accessible to the properly developed, individual human mind are, therefore, the characteristic of the development of our planet Earth, within this Solar system, and, within, thus, our galaxy.*

As a process of change, the abiotic aspect of our planet does not subsume life; and, organic life as such, as a principled process of change of the planet, does not subsume the creative powers unique to the human individual. Said otherwise, *man is in the image of the Creator,* a fact of which the poor heathen, President Obama, is to be described, like his pack of behavioral economists, as "utterly ignorant," as a pack of virtual yahoos from Gulliver's travels, when we are speaking in functional terms of reference, to his present social policies of practice as President.

However, that much said, the application of the immediately foregoing considerations, needs more careful examination. As a matter of convenience, compare the potential relative population-density of the human species, to that of systems representing, in turn, interacting systems of lower forms of life than mankind. The

contrast of man to ape, which is a matter of an absolutely categorical distinction, is illustrative.[10]

The Ironies of the Biosphere

Until the student has done a bit of a more serious sort of thinking about the nominal subject of the Biosphere, he, or she is, in most cases, about to be overtaken by certain highly relevant surprises.

Much of the mineral resource on which man's culture has depended for so-called "raw materials," thus far, upon such as relatively richer deposits of minerals, has often involved the depletion of the residues of earlier, relatively richer deposits which had been left behind, and concentrated as the residue of formerly deceased living processes. Thus, even the continued existence of the present levels of human population on Earth, depends upon those qualitatively higher levels of energy flux-density, per capita, and per square-centimeter cross-section, by means of which, we will be enabled to rely upon increasingly less richly concentrated mineral resources, but without loss of potential relative population-density per capita and per square kilometer of cross-section of the relevant process.

That is the most obvious of the leading practical distinctions of mankind from all lower forms of life.

Although living processes, as particular species, or sets of species, or living bio-masses of combined species and their varieties, have a creative (i.e., *noëtic, evolutionary*) power, relative to the non-living, they, too, are delimited by their depletion of resources which they employ. This is the case to such effect, that only the emergence of higher forms of life than those previously dominant, could ensure the attaining of even a relatively fixed, higher level of development of a biosphere. Only mankind, through willful inventions tantamount to discoveries of higher sets of universal physical principles, has been able to rise, willfully, above the relatively fixed potential of any non-human living species. Here lies the foundation of all competent notions of economy.

Among the elements of mankind's repertoire, we discover our potential for creating a quality of improvement in the Biosphere, which the Biosphere could not effect for itself.

---

9. This is what defines the health-care policies of the Obama administration as being axiomatically fascist. That a man regularly rode a donkey to work would not make him a jackass.

---

10. The ideologues of Silicon Valley are a case of creatures who have been self-defined as like the late Bertrand Russell devotees, the late Norbert Wiener and John von Neumann, as, professedly, not only sub-human, but virtually inorganic, not by birth, but by choice of profession. No wonder that Hilbert chucked each of that pair out of his Göttingen program for reason of their manifest incompetence.

The Crisis Among the Economists

People who are either charlatans, or innocently ignorant of the conceptions on which the notion of science depends, mistake mere statistics for science, in particular, and for truth in general. Thus, no statistician in any case known to me, has ever competently forecast the nature of a future, crucial quality of turning-point in the history of economies, on the basis of statistical method. As a matter of principle, he, or she could never succeed in such an attempt, however long he might attempt to do so.

All crucial turns in the U.S. economy, especially downturns, have come about through the intervention of what appeared, in retrospect, to most economists to date, and to most others, to have been unforeseen, and, for them, even virtually unforeseeable preconditions. However, since my own adoption of the successive standpoints of Gottfried Leibniz and (since January 1953) Bernhard Riemann's 1854 habilitation dissertation as the indispensable basis for a science of physical economy, I have presented a series of economic forecasts, beginning one in Summer 1956, chiefly for the U.S. economy itself. All of these forecasts have been confirmed by critical changes in the relevant course of events; in no case, have I encountered a competent substitute for my relevant forecast. In each case of comparisons which I have examined, the fault of my putative, and also failed rival has been, in each case, what proved to have been a fatal error of reliance on the commonly taught statistical presumptions of the academic, or comparable specialist.

This is not to suggest that there are no competent thinkers among the ranks of some parts of the economics and banking professions. However, so far, all economists whom I have known, even those I respect for their relative competence and related practical achievements, have failed to grasp the crucial principle which I present, and elaborate here. So, I have come to regard their competence, when it is expressed in some aspect of their work, as an essential part of, and contribution to my own intellectual constituency.

The point to be made can be fairly stated, as, that the recurring, professionally fatal error of my known opposing rivals in this profession, has been their expressed, virtually blind, Cartesian faith in a universe typical of the dupes of the "flat Earth"-like followers of Paolo Sarpi in general, and the followers of the brutish empire of the Physiocrats and, such among not only their own ranks, but also those plagiarists of the Physiocrats, such as Adam Smith and Jeremy Bentham.

In other words, in cases typical of my experience during the recent fifty years, the merely apparent successes obtained in the mapping of short-term intervals of action by linear methods, had often prompted unwarranted confidence in the Cartesian-like presumption, that to such effect, that what should have been recognized, as presently, as warning signs of a contrary longer-term development, were being overlooked, that as a result of what was implicitly assumed to be a passing anomaly, rather than a warning sign of the existence of an unpleasant, longer-term, underlying trend. *The usual expression of such foolish errors of assumption, was the always potentially fatal reliance on the stated, or implied presumption, that mere financial and related statistics, were the relevant evidence bearing upon defining the specific causes of trends in the underlying, real, physical economy.*[11]

The case of my successful short-term forecast, in mid-1956, of the February-March outbreak of the 1957 recession, is significant for our reference here, for reason of the nature of the systemic error by those who refused to foresee that crash as already imminent, as I had done.

In that case, the mid-1950s role of the same Arthur Burns which would be continued in the later triggering of the August 1971 crash of the U.S. dollar, done in concert with George Shultz, is exemplary.

Consider the case of the effort, like that of a cat covering its offal, to bury the stench created by that maladministration of the U.S. economy of the late 1940s, by that British stooge, President Harry S Truman, and after that, then by the new, Republican, Eisenhower administration. This situation led into a new consumer-spending form of the credit-bubble building-up under the man who would become Milton Friedman's sponsor, the same Arthur Burns.

Then, the intrinsically inflationary bubble of consumer-credit-led expansion, which occurred under Burns' influence, led quickly to such fraudulent practices as packing inflated prices of automobile dealer-

---

11. So, for example, a gain in nominal monetary wealth is frequently regarded as evidence of economic growth, even when this represents a contraction of the physical wealth of the economy. So, the Federal Reserve and other "bail-outs" unleashed under the lunatic, successive Bush and Obama Presidencies, since September 2007, have destroyed productive employment, physical output, standards of living, and have wiped out many formerly prosperous enterprises. Such lunacy is typical of that insanity known as "the magic of the marketplace."

ships' used-car trade-ins on new car sales. That inflation of new-car prices was done, in order to report pretended prices of what were actually heavily discounted new car sales, fraudulently, at prices either at list, or, increasingly, much higher than list. This bubbling, which was introduced, widely and wildly, into the financing of retail new car sales, was the bellwether of kindred swindles in the name of merchandising practices otherwise. Thus, the collapse of the market for the thirty-five-month-plus-thirty-sixth balloon-note variety of new-car sales, became a featured element of a general 1957-1958 recessionary collapse of the U.S. economy as a whole.

My experience, then, in having uttered what appeared to have been a uniquely successful forecast, a forecast of a February-March collapse of the U.S. economy into what became a deep recession at that time, provided me the clues for coming to understand the long-term waves of crisis which worsened over the course of the 1960s, long waves which led, thus, into the orchestrated, 1971 breakdown of the Bretton Woods system, and those following stages of ruin of the resulting economy, which occurred under President Richard Nixon and all of his successors in that office.

On this account, my response to the fact that nearly all evident professional rivals of mine had rejected my 1966-1971 warning of an oncoming breakdown of the existing, "Bretton Woods" monetary system, which I projected for a time at approximately the turn of the decade, and that this rejection persisted even after mid-August 1971, prompted me to challenge them as being "Quackademics." I challenged each and any among them to debate the issue of my success as compared with their manifestly systemic failure in their claims to be either "professional" or otherwise qualified as "academics" in this field.

So, eventually, in response to the continued, months-long pressure of my repeated charges of their having behaved as "quackademics," a debate was convened at New York's Queens College campus on December 2, 1971. That debate was between me and a then internationally leading professor of Keynesian economics, Professor Abba Lerner. That debate concluded with Lerner's rather plaintive statement, that, literally, "had the German Social Democrats accepted" Hitler backer "Hjalmar Schacht's" fascist "economic policies, Hitler would not have been necessary." Lerner was a close associate of New York University Professor Sidney Hook, who was a leader of the pro-fascist, post-World II Congress for Cultural Freedom (CCF). Neither that Fabian, nor Hook were pleased with my success in that Queens College debate.

That Queens College debate, had ended with a blush of shame-filled, momentary silence among the members of the faculty seated as spectators. The bitter warfare against me by the left-wing, pro-imperialist variety of fascists of the Fabian Society, such as today's onetime British Prime Minister Tony Blair, has continued with increasing virulence, ever since that time. After all, it was the British monarchy and England's Schachtmaster Montagu Norman, which had brought Adolf Hitler to power in Germany, all this with crucial assistance from the same Prescott Bush who was not only the father of U.S. Presidents George H.W. and the grandfather of George W. Bush, but also the true father of his son's and grandson's family political tradition.

So, as Hitler's Wehrmacht had overrun France, Britain had turned against Hitler and its own Neville Chamberlain, and had begun piteous begging for assistance from London's hated President Franklin D. Roosevelt, begging Roosevelt for rescue of an imperilled British Empire. Then, later, when Hitler's days were greatly foreshortened, and President Roosevelt had died, London's stooge Harry Truman, and the same Wall Street crowd which had backed Hitler during the 1930s, turned into a parade of the Franklin Roosevelt-hating, Wall Street kissers of the Royal British butt, once more, as in days of yore.

So, the crisis of today actually began on April 13, 1945, when President Harry Truman, by adopting the imperialist policies of John Maynard Keynes, which President Roosevelt had rejected, thus cancelled the most crucial of the axiomatic features of the general U.S. recovery which had been led by President Franklin Roosevelt up to that time. Truman's actions saved the British empire. Truman's wicked kissing of the British imperial butt, led, thus, to both the ruin of the U.S. economy, and into the threatened doom of civilization, globally, today. So, Truman's inauguration has led, consistently, to the generation of that economic crisis which was set into full swing by the corruption-riddled follies of Presidents George W. Bush, Jr. then, and Barack Obama now.

Then came the time, now, when I had been the only economist on the planet who had recognized, and warned, as in my July 25, 2007 international webcast, against the crisis which erupted immediately thereafter. I had proposed measures which could have brought this erupting

EIRNS/Stuart Lewis

LaRouche was the only economist on the planet, who had recognized, and warned, "as in my July 25, 2007 international webcast, against the crisis which erupted immediately thereafter. I had proposed measures which could have brought this erupting crisis under control...." LaRouche is shown here at a Jan. 17, 2008 webcast explaining his "Triple Curve" collapse function.

crisis under control. Those measures were prevented by the flagrantly corrupt actions of both the George W. Bush, Jr. and Barack Obama Presidencies, as by the relevant leaders of the houses of the U.S. Congress.

Through the continuing corruption, top down, of the relevant Presidencies and the culpable quotient among the leaders of the U.S. Congress, only those measures of reorganization in bankruptcy, which I had proposed during the course of July-September 2007, could have stopped the bleeding; those preventive measures have been willfully prevented under both those two Presidents and by the top leadership in the U.S. Congress.

Now that that Texas State Air National Guard hero George W. Bush, Jr. is no longer President, that same corruption is being continued now, in an even more insane form, by President Obama. Worse, that corruption is continued presently, with the added features of introducing exactly the same measures of crimes against humanity against the U.S. population itself, the same policies of genocide which Adolf Hitler had unleashed in September 1939.

There are relatively long, seemingly genetically-predetermined waves in the unfolding of history, from which come the virtual maelstroms which take the short-term optimists, like the sillier economists, unaware.

Such is the meaning of "ignorance is bliss." Such are the kinds of circumstances under which high-ranking fools realize their destiny as the great criminals of known history, such as the Roman emperor Nero, or the launching of Adolf Hitler by the Bank of England's Montagu Norman. Such are the consequences inherent in President Obama's current renewal of Hitler's practice of genocide.

What is driving that insanity which continues to drive U.S. national policy, now, top down? Or, more to the point, where is the remedy for this state of affairs?

A Crucial Lesson from Percy Shelley

The concluding paragraph of Percy Bysshe Shelley's **A Defence of Poetry** is devoted to what is, in point of fact, a thoroughly scientific definition of the roots of the *tensor*, that in the sense of Gottfried Leibniz's use of the concept of *dynamics*.

This conception, as presented by him, points out a key to understanding the current workings of world history.

Shelley focused attention on the fact that "the spirit of the age" embraces not only those who share that commitment in their own nature, but, also, sweeps up, into the tidal force of its embrace, many whose nature may be instinctively of a contrary quality. Such shifts, are familiar to us, from study of the behavior of members of the U.S. Congress, for example, that, over as recent an interval as the shift from the 2004 election-campaign, and throughout 2005, into the moral depravity which has largely dominated the proceedings in the Congress, since the beginning of 2006.

The tendency of some would be, to identify this as an expression of some dumb "herd instinct" among the legendary *hoi polloi*. The tendency shown, thus, often seems applicable to some whose evident moral world-outlook is like something scraped up from the late night barroom floor; but, I will confine my discussion of Shelley's referenced argument, here, to matters of a relatively nobler quality. I refer to *the category of social dynamics specific to any distinct culture of either a portion, or nearly all of a society.*

Such a phenomenon as treated in Shelley's **A Defence of Poetry** could not have been competently understood by a Rene Descartes, nor by the admirers of such moral and intellectual degenerates as Adam Smith and Jeremy Bentham. My intention in this matter can be understood, only from the standpoint of the *dynamics* of Gottfried Leibniz and the combined legacy of

Leibniz and J.S. Bach, as these influences were promoted, in turn, by the work and influence of one the greatest mathematicians and political figures of the Eighteenth Century, the Abraham Kästner (1719-1800) who was also the promoter of the development of Gotthold Lessing, and, thus, of the work of Lessing's collaborator Moses Mendelssohn. Such were the typical spirits of Shelley's own age. They created a wave, including our American revolution, which changed the course of history, in their time.

At this point in my account, it were efficient to introduce what might be regarded, mistakenly, by some, as a shift in the direction of the kind to which I am referring at this point. This shift in approach will avoid awkward "red herrings," and will soon turn out as stating a provable case respecting a very important, and most relevant, matter of principle, a principle underlying any competent science of economics.

Whereas, it is customary to fragment the conception of mankind, as by the presumption of a categorical, academic separation of what is called physical science, from Classical artistic composition, the fact of the matter is, as the discoveries of Kepler, Fermat, and Leibniz attest, that the specifically creative intellectual powers of the human individual in society, are located, not in mathematics, but in an extension to physical science met in both the role of *Classical irony* in poetry, drama, and in the methods of J.S. Bach, W.A. Mozart, Ludwig van Beethoven, through Brahms. The methods of metaphor, when transported from poetry and music into the practice of physical science, are the novel source for inspiration of physical-scientific and related achievements in increase of the productive powers of labor.

The following, partial explanation of that ironical fact, is required as a preliminary measure, at this juncture in both this present, and the following chapter of the report as a whole.

I begin by emphasizing, that the creative powers of the individual human mind, on which great revolutionary advances in knowledge of physical science depend, depend for their origins on a source which is uniquely specific to the human mind. This is a power which is lodged in the expressed role of creativity in Classical modes of artistic composition, such as Classical metaphor in poetry, drama, music, or the genius of Rembrandt's portrait of the insightful and lively Homer contemplating the silly fop portrayed as the virtually embalmed Aristotle.

There is no need to regard this ironical role of true creativity as mysterious. Academician Vernadsky helps us greatly in this specific matter. I explain this now, and, later, return, better prepared, to the great principle underlying Shelley's **A Defence of Poetry**.

The Abiotic, Biosphere & Noösphere

Man observes, and acts upon the Abiotic, the Biosphere, and the Noösphere. In the first two categories, the action is man's intervention, as if into domains from outside the mind of man *per se*. This practice is the principal ordinary location of the body of applied physical science; in this case, we are acting, with the mind, upon subjects other than the human mind itself. In the second category, in Classical modes of art, properly defined, the subject of practice is the subject of man's willful change in the quality of human behavior as such, as that point is aptly illustrated by reflections on the exemplary significance of J.S. Bach's books of forty-eight preludes and fugues, in which the structural composition of the willful development of space and time become a science of the singing mind.[12] Here, in the domain of Classical artistic composition, is the location from which human individuals' creativity moves changes of principle into the domain of the abiotic and biotic.

In all great Classical art, man, as the composer, remakes himself, by remaking the way in which he looks at both the world of the abiotic and the Biosphere, and also himself. The true expression of that quality of human creativity which sets man apart from all beasts, is found in what I now summarize here as the function of Classical artistic composition.

In that higher category of human individual experience, we are dealing directly with the manifestation of the specifically creative powers of the human mind. Consider the following, crucial quality of illustration of that point: the Leibniz infinitesimal. I describe the way the following issue came up, and then point out its relevance for the subject-matter to which I have pointed, immediately above.

Therefore, now consider the case of Leibniz's uniquely original development of the calculus.

Johannes Kepler left two very specific tasks to be treated by his successors. The first, is the concept familiar to us as the Leibniz "infinitesimal." The second was

---

12. One of the most convenient illustrations of this point is provided by the treatments by sundry great compositions derived from the precedent of W.A. Mozart's appreciation of Bach in his own K. 475 Fantasy. Each of these cases is unique; yet, they are consistent with the same principled idea.

The Abiotic: Dramatic rock formations on Santa Cruz Island in California; the Biosphere is making visible incursions.

The Biosphere: Garibaldi damselfish (Hypsypops rubicundus) *live around the Channel Islands.*

The Nöosphere: These young scientific investigators are exploring the tidepools at Moss Beach, in California.

"In all great Classical art, man, as the composer, remakes himself, by remaking the way in which he looks at both the world of the Abiotic and the Biosphere, and also himself. The true expression of that quality of human creativity [the Nöosphere] which sets man apart from all beasts, is found in Classical artistic composition."

the treatment of physical-elliptical functions, a challenge explored by notable contemporaries of Carl F. Gauss. In the matter of the "infinitesimal," once the ideological followers of Paolo Sarpi's Ockhamite Liberalism, considered Leibniz as safely deceased, a century-long effort was launched for the intended discrediting of Leibniz's discovery of the calculus. This was launched by the circles of the Venetian Antonio Conti and Voltaire. Those others most notably implicated in this anti-Leibniz hoax, included Abraham de Moivre, Jean le Rond D'Alembert, Leonhard Euler, and Euler's disciple, Joseph Lagrange.

The contribution of de Moivre to this anti-Leibniz hoax, was to suggest to his accomplice, D'Alembert, that the Leibniz infinitesimal was merely "imaginary," a mere fiction created by an inherent quirk in mathematics. Euler supported a slightly different sort of fraud; he insisted, in a letter to a German Princess, on the presumption of infinite mathematical divisibility. The myth of "imaginary numbers" came from these and related sources among the followers of Conti and Voltaire.

In his case, since Euler knew better than to add to the babbling about "imaginary numbers," his contribution to the hoax uttered by Conti and Voltaire, was

purely political opportunism, the fruits of which he passed on to his protégé Lagrange.

The genesis of these frauds against Leibniz, is to be traced, in modern European culture, to attacks on the work of, chiefly, such Leibniz predecessors as Filippo Brunelleschi and Nicholas of Cusa, and to the latters' part in defining "non-geometrical" curves such as the catenary. It is sufficient to note here that the catenary, or funicular curve, was employed as a physical principle of construction by Brunelleschi, as the physical principle of construction of his otherwise practically impossible crafting of the cupola for Florence's **Santa Maria del Fiore**. To similar effect, Cusa had insisted that Archimedes' professed quadrature of the circle, was a systemic error on the part of the followers of Archimedes. Cusa's follower Leonardo da Vinci had recognized the physical significance of the catenary and its functional relationship to the tractrix. The same type of significance lies with Pierre de Fermat's discovery of the principle of physical least action. Leibniz's development, in concert with Jean Bernouilli, of the universal physical principle of least action, superseding the earlier discovery of "quickest time" by Leibniz's friend Christiaan Huyghens, was fully established as the heart of Leibniz's refined version of his uniquely original, *circa* 1675, first discovery of the calculus, while working with Huyghens in Paris in such matters as the archives of Blaise Pascal.

The gist of the case is this.

From the outset, in its roots in Kepler's uniquely original discovery of the principle of universal gravitation, in his **The Harmonies of the World**, Leibniz's discovery of the calculus was rooted in physical, rather than merely formal-mathematical conceptions.

In point of fact, the matter was settled beyond further honest scientific debate, through the influence of a leading mathematician of the Eighteenth Century, Göttingen University's Abraham Kästner (1719-1800). As for the hoaxes attributed to black-magic specialist Isaac Newton, Newton's reputation was stripped down to virtually a net nothing by the successive, relevant work of the Ecole Polytechnique of Gaspard Monge, Lazare Carnot, and Alexander von Humboldt, and also, contrary to such as the attacks on them by the hoaxsters Rudolf Clausius and Hermann Grassmann, by the work of Gauss, Wilhelm Weber, Lejeune Dirichlet, and Bernhard Riemann in electrodynamics.

Said in other words, since the ancient science of *Sphaerics*, as in the work of the Pythagoreans and Plato, competent practice of geometry had been derived from physical principles of astronomy, and was practiced in a form fairly identified today as physical geometry. Today, for purposes of a science of physical economy, we should use "physical geometry" as a way of rejecting incompetent geometries, such as Euclidean geometry, just as we prefer the "physical chemistry" of Mendeleyev and Vernadsky, or the physical bio-chemistry of Vernadsky, to "physics."

The importance of such scrupulous uses of terminology lies, more simply, in emphasizing the experimental basis of knowledgeable practice in such fields of inquiry. We are properly obliged to insist upon such distinctions, since we do not actually know objects of sense-perception as such; we know the relevant phenomena as just that; we know the act of experiencing efficient control over relevant phenomena, through aid of what is experienced by some combination of our biological and synthetic instruments.

We are not nominalists on this account. We can know what we have experienced, and can identify existences as corresponding to such experiences; but, we step on our own feet if we presume that we can break the universe down into collections of objects, as the foolish Euclid did, when, in fact, our real knowledge is that of our human—*creative*—relationship to relations among processes, not things.

II. The Case of Shelley Continued: Why the Hoax Against Leibniz?

To locate the roots of the disaster which overtook civilization in the aftermath of the death of U.S. President Franklin Roosevelt, we must trace the germ of that cultural and economic disaster throughout a more than two-millennial span, since the Persian wars.

However, to be clear about these connections, we should begin this chapter, with a summary of developments prior to the decades-long wave of post-World War II cultural degeneration in trans-Atlantic society,

Who Is Satan?

If you were to wish that you knew who Satan is, you would study the footprints left by the reign of those satanic deities and the mortal monarchs who imitate them which preach a clearly satanic doctrine like that of "cap and trade" today. The essentially evil nature of those priests and preachers of existential despair is that they deny that the human individual is any better than just another beast. I do not wish to argue that the churches of today are that good; I do insist that the emptying of traditional churches is a reflection of a widespread moral degeneration, often identified as "existentialism," which gripped a leading stratum of the populations of the Americas and Europe born between approximately 1945 and 1958. The Obama Presidency's Larry Summers and his likeness among the so-called "Behaviorist economists" are exemplary expressions of the frankly pro-satanic influences produced as a current outcome of the moral degeneracy of the post-1945 existentialist insurgency of factions such as the Congress for Cultural Freedom, "information theory,' and the doctrine of **The Authoritarian Personality** of moral degenerates such as the "left-wing fascists" Theodor Adorno and Hannah Arendt.

—*Lyndon H. LaRouche, Jr.*

It was Leibniz who introduced the modern version of the dynamis of the ancient Pythagoreans and Plato, in his 1695 Specimen Dynamicum.

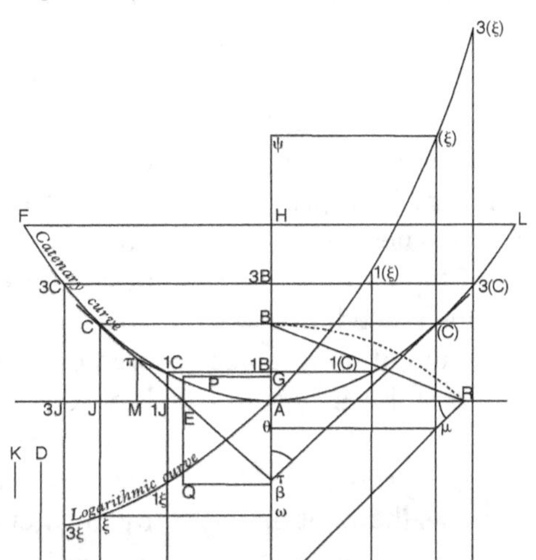

to a decline launched under the systemic moral and intellectual degeneracy typified by both the Congress for Cultural Freedom (CCF), in Europe, and the related influence of the specific cases of **The Authoritarian Personality** of such degenerates as Raymond Aron, and also the existentialists Karl Jaspers, Theodor Adorno, Martin Heidegger, Hannah Arendt, Herbert Marcuse, et al., who have, largely, destroyed the earlier, literate generations' sense of the interconnections between science and Classical competence.

Since that time, as death has peeled away, in succession, each generation which had been born during the last quarter of the Nineteenth Century and the first quarter of the Twentieth, the functional memory of what had once been actually Classical European civilization, was removed, largely by the combination of deaths and cultural attrition, generation by generation.[13] Such is the present nature and practical meaning of the terms *decadence*, or, for that matter, *degeneration*.

So, when the priests of ancient Egypt had spoken to their great visitor from Athens: "You have no old men among you," those Egyptians referred to the need for the preservation, and/or regaining of the experience of many successive generations of preceding times, as my own ancestry in New England is traced today to the experience of the first English settlements there. It is through long-reaching historical perspectives, perspectives rooted in the re-living of the actual experience of numerous, successive generations of one's predecessors, that we are enabled to acquire that sense of history which our U.S.A. of today has, unfortunately, virtually lost with the retirement from academic life of what had been the last surviving and competent American Classical historians, such as my late associate H. Graham Lowry.[14]

In the U.S.A. today, a past sense of actual history among what had been the actually literate rations of our population, has been replaced by the virtual disease of mere novelty, a novelty practiced as if for its own sake, not by historians, but the chronicles made up to fill the blank spaces with the mere commentaries on anecdotes. From among the leaders of our nation's intellectual life in earlier generations, real historians viewed history not as mere sequence of events, but of the deeply rooted, generations-long span of the internal life of society and its institutions, the long span of development under the ordered process of qualitative evolution of ideas. This was formerly seen as a process occurring within the framework of an evolving, long wave of progress in our nation's history since the original Massachusetts settlements.

That former grip on reality, has been lost, more and more, over the recent, increasingly decadent, post-World War II years. Except for landmarks and fragments of old memories which a few among us from that vicinity still share, State Street's Boston today is notable chiefly as a relic of its occupation by the slave-trad-

---

13. E.g. Franklin Roosevelt was born in 1882, whereas I was born forty years later; my parents' generation had mostly died out by the 1980s.

14. H. Graham Lowry, How The Nation Was Won: America's Untold Story, 1630-1754. (Washington, D.C.: Executive Intelligence Review, 1987)

ers and drug-traffickers of Lord Palmerston's British East India Company.

Against that background, the English Classical poet Shelley has a very special significance for today's true loyal patriot and statesman. If we take into account his work in poetry as such, his **A Defence of Poetry** is to be revered as his true testament, in fact, and, far more important, as a statement of a fundamental principle shared among the greatest poets and statesman of that time. That concluding paragraph of the latter writing, which I have already referenced in the preceding chapter of this report, has a very special kind of importance for our purposes in writing on the principles of a science of physical economy here.

The aspect of the process of *degeneration* and its *decadence,* which I am emphasizing as the fault of nations' recent practice, as contrasted to Shelley's work, is the role of today's virtual loss of the principle of *Classical poetic irony* on which the role of the actual creative powers of the mind of the individual in society depends. We have, to a very large degree, thus, virtually lost the intimate relationship to what had been the principles of Classical modes of musical and prosodic composition. It is this aspect of history which we, today, must view, in reading Shelley's **A Defence of Poetry**.

In respect to the historical antecedent for the subject of that writing, we must also emphasize the related significance of Shelley's own **Prometheus Unbound**.

This dramatic work was uttered by him as a proposed fulfillment of the essential intention of the last, apparently lost portion of Aeschylus' **Prometheus** trilogy. There, Shelley, echoing Aeschylus himself, grasps the most crucial fact respecting the full sweep of the known history of that known European history which spans three millennia's distance from Homeric times to the present day. It is this same theme which has gripped my attention and passions since, certainly, no later than my adolescent, flat rejection of the a-priorist features of Euclidean geometry, an adolescent experience which, in effect, destined me to come, in due course, to walk in the shadow of Bernhard Riemann.

Now, as to the importance of Shelley as a scientist:

In this present chapter so far, I have been accountable for relatively simpler aspects of this matter of history, which is to say, more immediate and elementary facts, facts which can be placed, more or less simply, on the table for discussion, as facts. However, when we take into account evidence that the human species has existed on this planet for probably not less than about one millions years to present date, we are confronted by the need to assess those kinds of evidence of cultural development of our species and its languages which are validated as being the footprints of what should have been known to us as history, but which are presented to us chiefly as only footprints, rather than as knowledge of the actual men and women who made them.

That lack of names from very ancient times, does not mean that an historian's studying such footprints of past cultures is to be deprecated as speculative. The historical implications of such evidence are to be discovered only with difficulty, but they should not be overlooked for that reason. As in all competent scientific method, we are searching for crucial pieces of evidence through which we bring the past to life, *dynamically*, as by the methods of criminal investigations of a scene of a recent crime, where investigations of such matters as footprints may lead to conclusive evidence as to who walked where and when, or even why. The method required, focuses upon the search for discovery of the needed, desired conclusions.

For this purpose, we must borrow from the practices of lapsed-time photography. We must do this, to shift the focus of our attention from a Cartesian-like series of isolated events, to search for possible *crucial, dynamic patterns of change in a kaleidoscopic quality of developments*. In other words, we are relying upon Leibniz's standpoint of *dynamics*, as opposed to Cartesian follies.

Such is the case with the matters presented in the immediately following account.

The Roots of Monetarism

The crux of Aeschylus' **Prometheus** trilogy, is the utterance by the play's most evil character, the Olympian Zeus, who had outlawed mankind's access to discovery of knowledge of the principle of "fire," just as the present generations of neo-Malthusians would, similarly, condemn nuclear power. On this account, the character of that Zeus is coherent with the account of the origin of the Olympians by the Roman chronicler, the Sicilian Diodorus Siculus. Up to that point, at the very least, the facts as stated by him are already solid basis for something like the investigation of a crime, or, some citizens would say today, an act of Congress under a corrupted Speaker Nancy Pelosi. That taken into account, the relevant, implied historical ground for Aeschylus' **Prometheus** trilogy, is, then, the following.

The most ancient mark of archeological distinction of the relics of an ape-like creature from an "early human" time, is the evidence of the associated use of fire. No higher ape monkeys around with fire, or nuclear power: only man. In Diodorus Siculus' chronicle, as traced to both Egyptian sources and to the evidence bearing on the subject of early Berber settlements, a portion of the legendary "peoples of the sea" brought their flotilla to settle at some part of, or near the northern coast of the territory of modern Morocco, where they colonized the already resident, relatively indigenous ancestors of the Berbers.

Then, and there, according to Diodorus, a parricide was conducted by the sons of the concubine Olympia, who was mated to the leader of that particular colony of the Peoples of the Sea. The parricides, led by the elder of those sons, the Olympian Zeus, came to play a dominant role among the maritime settlements which emerged in the rising waters along the coasts of the Mediterranean littoral, that from about the time of the inrushing waters from that sea, flooding what had become the transformation of a fresh-water lake into what is known presently as the Black Sea. All of this is fairly consistent with the setting of the known circumstances which are known from an Egyptian point of historical reference, from, broadly speaking, about that time.

Whatever Diodorus Siculus obtained from his contemporary sources, from inside Egypt or elsewhere, his account has fair consistency, as an impression, with the known developments leading into the Homeric accounts, as also consistent with the footprint of those antecedents known to have occurred in what archeology knows as the setting of the Peloponnesian War.

This brings our attention now, to a time when Plato, the successor of Socrates, was recently dead, when the then deceased Plato's nasty, wickedly reductionist, philosophical adversary, Aristotle, emerged as both a leading Greek influence in the circles of Philip of Macedon, and as the mortal adversary of the man who would become known as Alexander the Great. This was the same Aristotle who had been caught out as the principal among the conspirators who once unsuccessfully attempted assassination of Alexander the Great by Aristotle's method, poisoning, and who has been credibly suspected of authoring the later, successful attempt by poisoning.

As I have written in earlier locations, the situation in which Plato had emerged as a crucially significant figure in the making of future world history, is located

as following the judicial murder of Socrates, and, therefore, also after those ruinous effects of the Peloponnesian War which had led to the rise of King Philip's Macedon over a self-ruined Greece. The death of Alexander the Great, unleashed a system of rival oligarchical systems which were later fused as the Empire under Rome's (and the Isle of Capri's) so-called Augustus Caesar. What had tied that period of history together, from the outbreak of the Peloponnesian War to the reign of Augustus Caesar, was the rise of Mediterranean-centered monetarist imperialism in the wake of what had been the successive setbacks to, and later crushing of the Persian Empire. With that, imperial monetarist power shifted, clearly, to the cult of Plato's principal intended adversary, the Temple of Delphi, which had developed as the center of monetary imperialism of the Mediterranean and its littorals. Indeed, the Peloponnesian War itself had been essentially a struggle for supremacy between the two monetarist maritime powers associated with, and played by the treasuries and temple of the Delphi's Apollo-Dionysus cult.

Since the succession of the Roman and Byzantine empires, and the shift of the center of monetary imperialist power to medieval Venice, the systems of government in Europe itself have been dominated, to the present time, by offshoots of that Venetian imperial monetarist system which succeeded Byzantium as the principal monetary power of Europe. So, through the subsequent, February 1763 outcome of the "Seven Years" war, as through the times of the British-orchestrated Napoleonic wars, and since the great wave of world warfare centered on the Anglo-Dutch Liberal pivot, since the 1890 ouster of Chancellor Bismarck, through the collapse of the Soviet Union under London's Michael Gorbachev, the world at large has been dominated by the Venetian monetarist faction which came into being as the legacy of the founder of modern Anglo-Dutch Liberalism, Paolo Sarpi, a legacy which dominates Europe and its colonies, and semi-colonies, from around the world, still today.

The point to be emphasized here and now, is: *monetarism is the content of imperialism in the world today, just as London-centered Anglo-Dutch Liberal monetarism is the reigning power of the world, still, today.* Presently, the anti-science cult called "global warming," a fad organized by the World Wildlife Fund of Britain's Prince Philip, is not only an echo of the same anti-hu-

The death of Alexander the Great—murdered by Aristotle—unleashed a system of rival oligarchies, which were later fused as the Empire under Rome's Augustus Caesar. Left: Alexander (far left) defeats the Persian King Darius III (333 B.C.), in a fresco from Pompeii; right: Aristotle, in a detail from Raphael's "School of Athens" (1510), in Rome.

manist practices of an Olympian Zeus, as reported by Aeschylus' **Prometheus** trilogy, but expresses the same anti-human intent as had the legendary Olympian Zeus and the real-life Cult of Delphi.[15]

Similarly, when we hear, one more time, today, silly academics prating about European culture and its economic and parliamentarian attributes, we must be cautioned to think back to the onrush and aftermath of the Peloponnesian War, when the most essential, axiomatic presumptions of what became modern European economic and political culture were founded, founded, then as now, to be the expressed products of a reigning system of monetarist usury, under sundry political flags, to the present day.

Any, and every monetarist system is an imperialist system, under whose flag, money rules, as today, over the putative governments of nations, singly and collectively. That system controls. still today, that which controls a current President of our United States, who is controlled, presently, through the current agency of the British monarchy. That is the true nature of empire and imperialism, up through the present day. So, the implic-

itly treasonous actions of U.S. President Truman, beginning April 13, 1945, set into motion, then, what has become the threatened disintegration of our United States, and virtually all other nations, now. It is, thus, not "principalities and powers," as much as the long, long, conflicting waves of culture in all presently known history, or pre-history, which reign still over the nations of the world today.

The virtual secrets of each and all of the world's monetary systems today, are located centrally in that single fact. Thus, any attempt to maintain the precedents of monetary practices in western and central Europe since the death of U.S. President Franklin Roosevelt, is to be recognized, clinically, as a process of behavior-modifying conditioning of the collective minds and cultures of nations, their peoples, and their governments, since the death of Franklin Roosevelt, until today. The world at large has been, thus, as under the current U.S. President, and the worse British monarchy, a ship of fools, a captive of a hateful foreign power, a captive now en route to a threatened early death, that as a captive of the folly of a current wave of cultural despair.

In other words, *without eliminating the entirety of the world's present monetary systems, through instant reforms in national financial bankruptcy, into credit-systems based on the U.S. Constitutional model initiated by the first U.S. Federal Secretary of the Treasury,*

---

15. The cult of Delphi continued to be a leading power within the Mediterranean world, and the Roman Empire in particular, through the lifetime of its high priest and lying swindler Plutarch (of Plutarch's **Lives of Famous Men** notoriety). The site is a ruin today, but the evil spirit of its sophistry lives on, and reigns still over many of the leading minds of European culture still today.

Alexander Hamilton, there is no remaining possibility of saving the entirety of this planet from a general, physical breakdown-crisis of every and all nations of the world today.

If that ruin happens, it will be the present world monetarist system which has brought that calamity about.

The Cult of the Olympian Zeus

Silly, evil people teach the credulous, that money is power, and teach that the desire for money is the great incentive which moves the progress of society. That belief is a clever lie; it is not money, but the lust of some for power in, and over society, which reigns in such a fashion. Money is, after all, a mere fiction, which has no power of its own, but which is sometimes alleged to be a magical influence over those credulous enough to worship such a pagan god.

It is the existence of a private monopoly over the control of money, which is the evil which has brought down the once great United States, and which ruined Europe, over the decades since April 13, 1945, as happened, similarly, in many places during earlier times. It is only to the extent that money is made to be regarded as an essential component of political and related power over society, from the top, down, that money has reigning political authority. Today's popular fantasies aside, either the state shall reign over money, or money, as the truly alleged root of all evil, will reign above the institution of the nation state.

In all now globally extended history of European civilization since the onset of the Peloponnesian War, it has been systems of private control over the uttering and circulation of money, which have been the hallmark and essence of imperialist political systems.

The first relevant case which I chanced to examine in some depth, now nearly six decades ago, was the case of the self-inflicted decline of the cuneiform, so-called "bow tenure" culture of ancient Sumer, a non-Semitic colony of an Indian-Ocean based culture. The down-shift in the status of the farmers, which prompted them to neglect the need for desalination of irrigated plots, led to the cumulative ruin of the farmers' plots, as the quality of that culture shifted downwards, to virtual serfdom, and then a form of slavery. The use of relative poverty as an instrument of subjugation, and as a means to either the creation of systemic cultural obstacles, or even deep cultural regression, such as those of induced poverty, against technological progress, are typical of the roots of policies such as the ban, as by the Olympian Zeus of **Prometheus Bound**, on permitting the poor knowledge of the use of "fire," or nuclear power today, which is a characteristic expression of not only all oligarchical systems of rule, but of the promotion of virtually genocidal expressions of pro-oligarchical political-cultural tendencies in societies.

The modern remedy for such inherently imperialist character of the functioning of monetarist systems, has been chiefly the concept of national credit introduced as a prototype in the pre-1689 Massachusetts Bay Colony of the Winthrops and Mathers, and the embedding of that as a Federal constitutional principle in the founding of the U.S. constitutional republic. The strict limitation of the uttering of currency and related forms of credit to the national banking practices of the constitutional republic, as in the pre-1688 Massachusetts Bay Colony, and in the U.S. Federal Constitution, later, is both the only alternative to the inherent rapacity of monetarism, and for the dignity and defense of the sovereignty of all true republics.

At the present juncture in world affairs, only the virtually "over-night" replacement of a monetary system, by a state-credit system of each sovereign republic, could provide a way of escape from the presently on-rushing, essentially simultaneous global breakdown-crisis of all nations of the planet.

Thus, British Fascism Today

To understand the present world monetary crisis, we must know the historical roots of the phenomenon of fascism, as being, essentially, a British creation which was introduced, famously, to nations such as post-World War I Italy and Germany, among other locations. Fascism was then introduced only from London, as in the cases of both Benito Mussolini and Adolf Hitler personally. Fascism, as it had been known as *synarchism* under that British puppet, Napoleon III, earlier, has always been used as a device employed by the British imperial control of the international monetary system, where it provided a form of dictatorship employed to bring about, and suppress the resistance to both national and international monetarist interests, which is an inherently natural inclination of those populations which have become acclimated to the notion of modern nation-state republics such as our own United States.

Fascism is, for exactly that reason, the leading thrust

"To understand the present world monetary crisis, we must know the historical roots of the phenomenon of fascism, as being, essentially, a British creation ... introduced, only from London, as in the cases of both Benito Mussolini and Adolf Hitler personally." Here: The Duke and Duchess of Windsor are warmly greeted by their "hero," in 1937.

of the British monarchy's global policies under the present conditions of global monetary crisis, in a present time when the existential interests of the citizens of the U.S.A., and relevant other nations, have come into a state of inevitable conflict with the monetarist form of international financier interests, as we have experienced such a treasonous act by some members of the U.S. Congress, since about September 2007.

To understand this significance of modern fascism, we must see it as introduced to Nineteenth-century France under the installed British puppet Napoleon III, as under such rubrics as synarchism, then, or, later, as Twentieth-century fascism. It was brought into Twentieth-century Europe, and beyond, by the British Empire of the time of Lord Palmerston and Queen Victoria as part of the reactions of the British Empire to the defeat of Lord Palmerston's puppet, the Confederacy, at the hands of U.S. President Abraham Lincoln. The purpose then, was to halt the surge of influence radiated from that U.S. victory into the leading circles of continental Europe.

Later, the synarchist model was exported from France into Italy, in the form of the Mussolini dictatorship. That latter dictatorship, was, for example, like Benito Mussolini himself, a British puppet, ushered into

power by a British agent of Venetian pedigree, Volpi di Misurata.[16] Adolf Hitler was a creation of the Bank of England's Montagu Norman, and also Norman's Wall Street partners in Brown Brothers Harriman. The British dumped their Hitler, Mussolini, and other continental European fascist clients, *which they had created, only* when London saw the Wehrmacht crossing Germany's western border in France; with the fall of France, London then came screaming to Britain's hated adversary, President Franklin Roosevelt, for rescue, out of fear that the addition of France and its navy to Hitler's forces would mean the end of the British empire.

Since the death of President Franklin Roosevelt, we have been confronted by a new variety of fascism, even more deadly to civilization as a whole, than Hitler. The greatest present threat to all humanity is, now, the particularly nasty oligarchical specimens launched as the Bilderberger cult headed by the Malthusian pair of Britain's Prince Philip and the Nazi-SS veteran Prince Bernhard. Prince Philip and his Queen, still today, are among the most wicked people in the world, on just this account.

To understand that Prince Philip better, compare the rabidly, mass-murderously Malthusian policies of Prince Philip with the identically mass-murderous sentiments shamelessly asserted by the late Bertrand Russell, who is fairly described, as by some well-informed

---

16. Count Giuseppe Volpi di Misurata had operated as a key British agent deployed, from London under what emerged as British Fabian control like the similar case of British agent Alexander Helphand ("Parvus"), into the British Empire's "Young Turk" venture; "di Misurata" was a supplement to his name which Volpi had acquired in commemoration of a special service to a British enterprise in which he was engaged following his Young Turk engagement. During much of the 1930s, Mussolini enjoyed the patronage of the same Winston Churchill who, presently at the Italian border of Switzerland, was to supervise the deaths of both Mussolini and Carla Petacci, who were fleeing for a supposedly intended meeting with a much-embarrassed Churchill at that Swiss border. "Parvus," a case similar to that of Volpe, had also been recruited into the service of the British Fabian Society during a crucial visit to London, including a meeting with the aging British Fabian asset Frederick Engels during the 1890s. Among Helphand's roles in British service, he was a professional gun runner for British munitions interests, and an organizer of local wars to match. He, like Volpi, ended up as a fascist agent, but one operating in Germany, rather than Italy, at the time of his demise.

circles, as outranking even Adolf Hitler as the single most thoroughly evil person of the Twentieth Century. The satanic Prince Philip has been a relative amateur in evil, compared to the virtual Grand Inquisitor out of the pages of Dostoyevsky, Bertrand Russell.[17]

The faction of the United Kingdom led by the British royal family, is openly controlling the U.S. Obama Presidency at this present time, a Presidency which was created by that British monarchy, with the special complicity of the British monarchy's current special agent, former British Prime Minister Tony Blair.

This corrupted Presidency is, for the moment, the entity which aims to impose a health-care practice today, which is modelled on the war-time Adolf Hitler design for eliminating "lives not worthy to be lived."

In brief, the current policy of President Barack Obama, is the fascism of Prince Philip's World Wildlife Fund, the goal of which the Prince has declared to be, that of reducing the present world population from the present approximately six and a half billions souls, to less than two: *that genocide is the real purpose of the efforts to steer U.S. President Barack Obama by his British masters*.

The "green" genocide program which Prince Philip has frankly set forth for the targeted population of the U.S.A., among other nations, could not be installed under a truly democratic government. For applying such goals to a modern democratic form of nation-state, the Roman imperial tradition, now called "fascism," has been prescribed. For the U.S. people and its governing institutions, time is now rapidly running out, unless President Obama's genocidal health-care program is uprooted now.

For the British monarchy's present intentions, the anti-nuclear, "Green" fascism already adopted by the Nazi Party of the late 1920s, is prescribed. The key for understanding this is to be found in the study of Aeschylus' **Prometheus Bound**.

Fascism & Genocide Are British, and Green

To come most directly to that point, without the proliferation of the development of nuclear fission as a primary source of power, the presently leading problems of nourishing the population of this planet can not be solved in a timely way. The standard sort of fanatical opposition to nuclear power, is, frankly, one which requires the fanaticism of a brainwashed constituency of the type already all too abundant inside the United States, as in Europe. This sort of fanaticism serves the purpose of the brain-washers in the same sense of intention as the banning of fire by the Olympian Zeus of **Prometheus Bound**.

It is by no means nuclear-fission power alone which is the British empire's concern in this matter. The significance of the proposed nuclear ban has been twofold.

First: nuclear-fission technologies are not only the basis for a high-technology economic culture, but are an urgently needed demand as a unique solution for the tasks of maintaining and raising the level of employed technology and products. Without such technology, the world is already running out of the supplies of such things as the drinkable cheap water on which decent life depends.

Second, from the camp of the evil: To achieve the social-political goals of the fascist recipes which the British monarchy's present policies intend, it is considered necessary to turn back the clock of progress in all heretofore industrialized nations, as the London-steered Anglo-American faction deliberately destroyed the economy of Mexico in August-October 1982 and beyond. Not only Mexico's then-active nuclear power development, but the entire sweep of industrial and infra-structural development,

As any competent physical chemist can demonstrate conclusively, the increase of the potential relative population-density of mankind, even the maintenance of a present level of such potential, depends upon a secular trend of increase in the energy-flux density of sources of power as this increase is reflected in the characteristics of the periodic table of physical chemistry.

The existence of life on this planet depends actually upon the role of increased supplies of carbon dioxide in the system, a supply which is used by sunlight (chiefly) through the marvelous role of the pollywog-looking chlorophyll molecule. That is, chlorophyll's characteristic action is both to collect the power of solar radiation in its antenna-like "tail," and then transform that power, through an increase in its relative, effective energy-flux density, for the production of the principal bio-chemical elements upon which the existence of the Biosphere depends. Nothing could be more insane, scientifically, than covering over what should be developed as areas of biomass, by covering vast areas of landscape with

---

17. Russell destroyed more minds, including those of notable scientists, than he succeeded in doing with the actual body counts which have been the fruits of his influence on policies. On Russell, Josef Stalin's judgment was right, and Khrushchev a dubious character.

inherently wasteful systems of solar panels and windmills operating at very low energy-flux-densities. The scientifically soft-headed schemes for the conversion of solar radiation, at a lower energy flux-density than the work by chlorophyll, into the biomass on which human life, among other matters, depends, is not only stupid, but implicitly a crime against humanity.

The purpose of a biofuels policy is not production of power, but increased rates of killing of people, as President Obama's current combination of health-care plus energy policy attests to this intended effect.

In the physical-chemist's history of our planet, it has been the up-shift in energy-flux-density in the types of sources of applied power employed, on which the continued existence of mankind depends for maintaining the human population even at its present levels. Without the power of modes of nuclear fission associated with uranium- and thorium-based nuclear fuels, the planet is now threatened with a general catastrophe.

The purpose of the British imperial policy of "green genocide" pushed by the allies of evil Prince Philip and his creepy son, Charles, is not merely to stupefy and brutalize the people, but to shorten the life-span in ways which conform to relatively unskilled, labor-intensive modalities, and to further this policy by the practice of measures designed to, so to speak, "cull the herd" of those who have passed the age recommended for a relatively unskilled labor-force whose employment is chiefly engaged in labor-intensive occupations which a middle-aged person might find "too strenuous to keep up." For deeper insights into the British monarchy's present motives, examine the utopian novels of such protégés of the trio Aleister Crowley, H.G. Wells, Bertrand Russell, and the subject of ergotamine, as presented by the examples of Aldous Huxley and George Orwell.

Prince Philip's shamelessly stated, pro-satanic intention, is not only to halt and reverse scientific and

Prince Philip see human population growth as the "single most serious long-term threat to survival.... If it isn't controlled voluntarily, it will be controlled involuntarily by an increase in disease, starvation and war," he told People *magazine, in 1981.*

technological progress, but to degrade the population of the entire planet into a state of brutishness in which a stupefied and greatly reduced human population lacks the degree of development of its culture and its intelligence through which mankind might rise again above the crudest imaginable degree of slavish brutishness, a brutish state in which, as Bertrand Russell explained, young people "are able to procreate more freely," while impassioned by the pleasures of their cultivated, brutish, stupidity, but older people, and the sick shall die sooner, and also quicker, as the economic advisors of that British asset and U.S. President Obama have demanded.

Prince Philip's Fascism in Action

A related, specifically fascist type of assault on humanity generally, is expressed as the elimination of national sovereignties by the mode of imperialist tyranny known as "globalization." Essentially, no nation shall grow its own food, or exert sovereignty over the technologies it employs. At the same time, "globalization" of the labor-force lowers the level of technology at the population's command to a virtual condition of pauperized peonage.

Similarly, the most valuable minds in a population are those matured layers which represent accumulated, mature knowledge. If you wish to lower the effective "intelligent quotient" of a population, lower the level of life-expectancy of the population through the aid of measures akin to those of Adolf Hitler's "Tiergarten Vier (T4)" health-care policies. Even the HMO policies of practice introduced under the Nixon Presidency are already doing much evil in that direction.

Such policies as those degrade the victimized population to brutish levels of intellectual and cultural life, just as the Roman systems of serfdom and slavery did, and as preventive measures expressed as mass murder against "uppity" parts of the subject populations, or by religious wars and pogroms organized among differing portions of the subject Roman or Byzantine empires or the feudal organization of Europe under Venetian monetarist direction.

The adoption of the model of the Roman Emperor known as Julian the Apostate, by the British East India Company's Lord Shelburne, was a choice made essentially as an expression of author Edward Gibbon's quirkish playfulness. The fact is, that the Roman imperial system was permeated by its practice of strategies such as those of Julian, from the start to finish. The exact same policies of "divide and rule" are practiced, as by perpetual Israel-Arab conflict, always arranged by the British Empire, as in that domain of Sykes-Picot as the so-called "Middle East," today.[18] So, the empire of the British East India Company was established at the February 1763 Peace of Paris. The British Foreign Office's imperial power was affirmed by a new "Seven Years War" conducted by Napoleon Bonaparte, wittingly or not, on behalf of Britain's zeal to secure its imperial grip over all continental Europe.

Chancellor Bismarck, then already ousted, identified what was to become known as World War I as "a new 'Seven Years War.'" The entire span of warfare from the time coinciding with the destabilizing effect of the 1894 assassination of France's President Sadi Carnot: the launching of Japan's 1894-1945 warfare against China, Korea, and Russia, and the 1941 Japan attack on Pearl Harbor, were each, and all organized by Japan's 1920s agreement with Britain.

Actually, there was no real break in global warfare following Versailles. There were only virtual siestas used for preparing new outbreaks of mass killing. So, the Versailles Treaty was the occasion for the organizing of the march into the next world war intended, initially, to be a naval assault by the combined forces of Britain, Japan, and others, with Japan assigned then, already during the 1920s, for taking out the U.S. Pearl Harbor naval base.

Similarly, in September 1946, Bertrand Russell announced the British intention to prepare a nuclear attack on the Soviet Union, an attack intended by him to "establish world government." Russell's proposal then, should be used as a point of past reference for examining the probable intention of the unspeakably evil,

former British Prime Minister Tony Blair today. Will the current policies, and an existentialist sense of mortal urgency gripping the aging Prince Philip today, combined with the reckless ambition of former Prime Minister Tony Blair, lead to an early explosion of escalation into even thermonuclear warfare, perhaps using some lunatic and desperate Israeli government as, perhaps, Tony Blair's toy, to trigger that holocaust?

Before resuming the treatment of the strategic role of Percy Shelley's thesis we should prepare the way for that in the following way.

In working to destroy Classical culture, the authors of the global cultural-paradigm shift of the post-World War II decades, have not merely destroyed that degree of political sanity existing among leading nations, which had existed during the period of both the U.S. entry into the first and second so-called world wars. With deaths' weeding out of the ranks of what had been the relatively saner layers of the leading political and military leaders of nations during the course of the two post-war decades, and with the relatively greater calamity of the rise toward a presently dominant political role of the "68er" generation, we have lost much of the factor of sanity provided by Classical culture which would have prevented such an atrocity as something like a Blair's unleashing the madmen in the Israeli establishment for launching a "preventive attack," in the interest of the British Empire, perhaps even a nuclear-weapons attack on Iran. After all, it is the imperial British establishment which actually controls its Sykes-Picot puppet, the Israeli establishment, not the people of Israel. Such an enterprise would probably wipe out most of the Israeli population, but as Bertrand Russell wrote of such British enterprises:

> "But, bad times, you say, are exceptional, and can be dealt with by exceptional methods. This has been more or less true during the honeymoon period of industrialism, but it will not remain true **unless the increase of population can be enormously diminished**. . . . War, so far, has had no very great effect on this increase, which continued through each of the world wars … perhaps bacteriological war may prove more effective. If a Black Death could spread throughout the world once in every generation, survivors could procreate more freely without making the world too full. …This state of affairs might be somewhat unpleasant, but what of it? Really

---

18. "Organizing a league of sports teams" is more accurately identified as "conditioning players and spectators alike to participate in exhibitions of divide-and-rule." Hence, the impassioned spectators are not accidentally known as "fans" ("fanatics"), and, certainly, British religious warfare is rehearsed, in spirit, on the proverbial "playing fields of Eton."

high-minded people are indifferent to happiness, especially other people's...."[19]

The possibility of chaotic warfare, under conditions of a planetary breakdown-crisis of the type now threatened, is the most notable of a variety of likely cases in which the London-managed Sykes-Picot cockpit could be deployed as a detonator of a Balkans-like eruption of more general international military and related conflict.

Most among the relevant powers who might lead in such a general war, as the U.S. itself, have, recently, already wasted away their former capabilities for non-nuclear, regular warfare. Presently, as we witness in President Obama's wild insanity expressed in an escalation of war in Afghanistan, or the current Israel government's emphasis on its right to launch war against Iran, small frictions can spark great fires, even totally wild ones. Small, childish minds are playing with very big, and deadly, toys. After all might be considered, virtually no government of the world can be considered, now as predictably capable of sanity, if brought to the trigger-point of a general crisis.

To put the same point another way, the essential consideration in warfare is the capability of the warrior for recognizing and conducting the kinds of continuing action called "peace."

Today's Awful Nightmare

Consider the scarcely irrelevant case of the present United States of America. There are sane and capable elements in the institutions of the U.S. Federal government, but, unfortunately, they are not securely in current actual control of the way the Obama government as a whole would react. Among the most worrying features of that situation, is the manifest, rampant immorality, which has been mustered since July 2007 for the purpose of doing nothing, as the government as a whole, which would be, actually, a sane response to an important general, even existential quality of crisis.

In the meantime, the rest of the world is in a comparable state of mind.

Solutions to grave crises require sane persons in charge. We have no assurance of that quality as being available from the Presidency, or the U.S. Congress at this time, under that British puppet, President Obama, on down. Other aspects of the Federal government, yes:

but they are not yet in an assured position to carry out viable options.

The rest of the world does not appear to be in a much better current state of mind, at its top, than the British monarchy's President Obama. Examining the reports received showing the exhibited state of mind of leading figures in crucially important places of authority, one thinks of peeking into the offices of crucially important officials, expecting to find the occupant sitting naked in a plastic bathtub in front of his, or her desk, making giddy sounds between moments of blowing bubbles.

The persons in question may know something they would have done, normally, to deal with the immediate problem at hand, but they know, presently, that they would not be permitted to do it, under current new, London-dictated, Obama rules. Therefore, when all else fails, if you are a crucially important official, and you are not able to actually go insane, the best advice is that, if you intend to keep your position, you, at least, pretend to do so.

In short, the situation among the ranks of the top commands, is presently clinical.

When this happens, you know, if you are sane, that what you had considered "the system," has come to its end. If so, you then know, that something suddenly very new, is urgently required. That is where my role comes in.

III. Dynamics & Shelley

We now come to the matter of the nature of human scientific and related creativity as such.

To enable the reader to grasp the significance of Percy Bysshe Shelley's **A Defence of Poetry,** for the purpose of understanding the role of human creativity in physical science and economics, here, we must resume my earlier emphasis on Gottfried Leibniz's introduction of the modern version of the *dynamis* of the ancient Pythagoreans and Plato, as I had already done in identifying both Leibniz's 1692 exposure of the fraud in the method of Descartes, and Leibniz's introducing the related conception of modern *dynamics*, in his 1695 **Specimen Dynamicum**.

To begin the exploration of that discovery by Leibniz, here, the essential distinction of the conscious and semi-conscious powers of actual individual human creativity, the distinction from the behavior of all lower forms of life, must be located in certain specific qualities of discovery of universal physical principles, such

<hr>

19. Bertrand Russell, **The Impact of Science on Society** (1953), emphasis added.

as the matter of Leibniz's **Specimen Dynamicum**.

This discovery by Leibniz, was one which had depended, in turn, upon the method employed in Johannes Kepler's preceding, uniquely original discovery of the principle of universal gravitation, as presented in his **The Harmonies of the World**. That later discovery by Kepler, is, as I shall show here, of crucial importance for showing the role of his method, as underlying the proper definition of both the actual principles of economy, and important, closely related matters.

My own treatment of the relevance of Kepler's work for a science of physical economy, here, is, essentially, an outgrowth of what was put on the table by Albert Einstein's treatment of the subject of the *tensor*, not only from the standpoint of the work of Bernhard Riemann, but also that of what I have referenced here as the earlier discoveries of Kepler. As I have stated here in an earlier chapter, we must also emphasize Academician V.I. Vernadsky's correction of Einstein's own treatment of the subject of the *tensor*, that from a relatively still higher vantage-point in experimental scientific method, than had been employed by Einstein himself.

Before carrying the discussion of the subject of the tensor itself a step further, I take the precaution of restating my own point of view on the role of that modern scientific method, from Cusa through Einstein and Vernadsky, in defining a science of physical economy, as I have identified that subject in the preceding chapters of this present report.

The Failure of Empiricism

The popular, but mistaken approach to the subject of science, which is encountered in both popular, and much scientific opinion, still today, rests on the misguided presumption that sense-perception is in some immediate relationship, in and of itself, to what are, in fact, the merely presumed realities which some might

Percy Bysshe Shelley, in his "Defence of Poetry," identifies "the spirit of the age" as that which "embraces not only those who share that commitment in their own nature, but, also, sweeps up, into the tidal force of its embrace, many whose nature may be instinctively of a contrary quality."

wish to associate with the notion of "self-evident" sense-experiences. The *a-prioristic* presumptions associated with the schoolbook teaching of Euclidean geometry, are typical of that erroneous, systemic form of incompetence which is so frequently spread in the teaching of what passes, even still today, for the underlying assumptions which have been more or less forcefully imprinted upon an education which, itself, has been conducted for such anticipated uses as the preparation of the student for exposure to what are considered various scientific matters, and also the teaching of economics.

Under the influence of such relatively popular, but erroneous opinion as that, the mathematical and related formulations usually taught as statements of experimentally proven principles, in economics, or otherwise, have been widely presumed to be a more or less authoritative type of a merely mathematical statement of a universal physical principle. This has been the source of the inherently socio-pathological characteristics of a traditional practice by the Anglo-Dutch Liberal empiricists-behaviorists trained in the tradition of the British East India Company school of imperialism, that by the followers of Adam Smith and Jeremy Bentham.

In my own opposition to such, and kindred a-prioristic presumptions as those which I have already listed in preceding chapters here, we must consider the evidence to the effect, that since the human biological faculties which we regard as the instruments of sense-perception, may be just that, that the relatively more popular notions of space, matter, and time, are merely shadows cast upon the mind, that according to the inhering, systemic peculiarities of the given senses. *However, the related paradox is, that they are usually real shadows.* In that view of the matter, which has been my own long-standing view since my adolescence, *the challenge of the very name of science, most emphatically, impels us to make the assumption, that our task is to discover what it is which has cast those shadows which we have experienced as sense-perceptions.*

All among those whose names which I cherish today as representing the greatest scientific minds of known ancient through modern intellects of science and art, have manifestly confronted this same challenging question within themselves. Shelley's proposition, summed up in the concluding paragraph of his **A Defence of Poetry** *poses that same question, not only for poetry, but, also, implicitly, for physical science. This convergence of the principles of Classical artistic composition on the principles of physical science, is the crucial subject-matter with which any actually competent science of physical economic behavior must be occupied today, as I am, here.*

That issue, as I have thus just posed it in this way, places *the actual existence* of all truly universal principles outside the presumed habitat of merely mathematical formulations. For that case, Kepler's famous discovery of a mathematical formulation for the organization of a composed Solar system, as the mathematical results of his work, which were plagiarized by the synthesizers of the scientific reputation of the black-magic specialist Isaac Newton, gave us a true representation of the *shadow* of the universal principle involved, but that formulation itself is not, and was not the *ontological actuality* of that principle: human footprints are not people.

Kepler's solution, on which all competent teaching and practice of European physical science since has depended, *depends upon a consideration which lies outside the presumptions associated with the characteristics of both the notion of the nature of the mere perceptions of respective senses of sight and sound.*

That point which I have just stated here, is exactly that kind of point made by Albert Einstein on the implications of Kepler's uniquely original discovery of universal gravitation. *This is also the fundamental, underlying principle of all competent practice of a science of physical economy.*

In Einstein's case, he defines Kepler's discovered principle as, at first stroke, as appearing to bound the universe, as if externally, but also systemically. He also presumes that, therefore, the universe as a whole, while extremely large, is, nevertheless, also *finite in principle*, rather than truly infinite *mathematically*. The question which arises immediately from these considerations, is the question: *is there "an outside" for this universe? Is there "another universe, outside our own?"* Einstein

says, "No," and there are excellent reasons, for agreeing with him on that latter point.

To make the point clearer: the presumption concocted by such hoaxsters as Rudolf Clausius, Hermann Grassmann, Lord Kelvin, et al., which is known as the claimed principle of reductionist thermodynamics, the so-called principle of entropy (or, "second law" of thermodynamics), was an ontological fraud from its inception. Clausius and Grassmann claimed to have derived their argument from the work of Lazare Carnot's nephew, Sadi Carnot; but, that report by Grassmann et al., as defended, gratuitously and maliciously, by the editor of Riemann's own collected works, was also fraudulent methodologically, as that is demonstrated in a study, following the work of Ampere, which was prompted by Carl F. Gauss, and conducted through proof-of-principle experiments in electrodynamics which were conducted at Göttingen University under the direction of Wilhelm Weber, that with the relevant cooperation of Lejeune Dirichlet, Riemann, and Kohlrausch.

The universe is, in fact, anti-entropic, as this is illustrated dramatically by the achievements of Academician V.I. Vernadsky for physical biochemistry. Kepler's universe is finite, but unbounded.[20]

So, as I have pointed out earlier in this present report, true universal physical principles lie as if "outside" the territory of the naive presumptions of the true believer, outside a certain notion of a universe which is wrongly presumed to be in perfect congruence with the naive presumptions of sense-certainty. *As Kepler's uniquely original discovery of gravitation shows, all truly universal physical principles exist outside that domain of any mathematics which is congruent, in itself, with the crude notions of sense-certainty.*[21] The mathematical expression of such principles, is presented, in each instance, as a shadow of the implied principle, rather than being what might be regarded as the efficient action of the principle as such.

What I have said, up to this point, in this chapter thus far, begs an additional question. This question is crucial for any competent attempt at an actual science of physical economy. The crucial ontological question so posed, is: *What is, ontologically, the efficient form of the action upon the universe by the principle of true*

---

20. This is the same argument made by Philo of Alexandria against the a-priorist arguments of the Aristoteleans of Philo's own lifetime.

21. Thus, any competent physical geometry is anti-Euclidean.

human creativity? Merely to ask that question, is equivalent to challenging still popular assumptions respecting the nature of the difference between willful man and the beasts. All competent attempts at a scientific notion of economy, depend absolutely on accepting, and also finding the answer to that specific question.

Perhaps You Are Now Shocked!

I shall now probably shock you a great deal more.

In my experience with these conceptions which I have just outlined in this present chapter, so far, I have found that the usual cause of the inability of many who could be regarded as, otherwise, literate, professionally qualified minds, is that even all of the evidence to which I have referred categorically thus far, would fail to equip them to grasp the implications of this matter in a practically efficient manner. That fault actually lies not so much with their choice of subject-matter as such, as within themselves.

I explain.

The source of that stubborn problem which they have experienced in that fashion, is their defective sense of the location of that entity which they associate with their notion of their referent for the concept "I," their notion of the ontological location of that "I." Therefore, to grasp those conceptions which are indispensable for coming to understand the subject of economy in an efficiently sensible way, there must be a certain, definite kind of shift in the subject individual's sense of "the location of" a sensed personal identity, a shift which I recognize as expressed in the work of a number of scientific minds, such as Einstein himself.

The essential problem which confronts us in that apparent paradox, is that, firstly, universal physical principles are not themselves sense-objects *ontologically*. Nevertheless, they are efficient. All competence in defining universal physical principles, depends upon this consideration.

Ask, therefore, is the scientist's, or economist's sense of a personal identity located within the notion of sense-certainties, or are the senses to be recognized as lying within the bounds of a domain of the mere shadows presented to the mind of the thinker? All practical competence in economics depends upon insight into that specific consideration.

Those who have succeeded in dealing more or less competently with this conceptual problem which I have just outlined in that way, will have effected a shift in the location of their sense of identity as a thinking person.

The nature of the challenge which they must conquer, in themselves, is located in the way they think of their own identity as a thinking being, rather than as another object in the domain of sense-perception.

To wit:

The customary source of the usual failure of the subject type of person being criticized here, is his, or her strong emotional attachment to a naive sense of personal, social identity, a sense rooted in strong attachment to the power which something more potent than their mere, personal sense-perception of the world exerts, as in the course of defining their sense of identity as a person.[22]

Stated in other words, how could they consider offending what other people see in them, in respect to their character as a mere object of sense-perception, as an object of the type which might be seen as mere objects, by onlookers, through the faculties of mere sense-perception as such.

To put that point about as bluntly as it deserves: they are being neurotic.

They are neither "seeing" the identity of the person, their actual selves, inside the relevant sense-perceptual object, and, often, in most encounters, they simply could not care less. They tend, thus, to regard the other person as primarily an object of perception, and to recognize something deeper than that mere object, if only by more or less rare exception.

In dealing with this rather commonplace problem, which is faced by any competent management, or similar consultant, for example, the relevant professional, if actually competent, looks past the external features, into the relatively principled characteristics operating

---

22. I call the reader's attention to the legendary case of the type of man who is widely regarded as a virtual tower of competence in his profession, but a pitiable failure, even a virtual case of born-again childishness at home. In modern business enterprises and comparable occupations, the leader often enjoys the advantage of playing a virtual game, where he is protected from reality by rules like those of the make-believe life of the sports playing-field. He or she enjoys the protective cloak of an assumed, role-playing identity. He, or she, is thus protected, by the definitions of his duties, authorities, and responsibilities, from the risk of full moral accountability for the outcome of his, or her, own behavior for society as a whole. His belief in his success in that role, protects him, psychologically, by means through which he is permitted to believe are the rules of the game he is playing, protects him from assuming accountability for the effect of that role-playing on the real world he inhabits. Back home from work, he is often the victim of a reversal of the definition of reality; now, what he brings "home," from work, confronts him. The outcome is therefore often, in principle, tragic, not only for the individual and the family, but even, sometimes, for our republic.

from behind that mask worn by the person who would be considered, otherwise, as merely a sensory object: *the real person, existing in the eyes of true insight. Otherwise, he or she is not a competent consultant in matters of economic management, and not really professionally qualified as an economist, either.*

One must view oneself, that very critically, with the same insight. It is precisely that insight—truly compassionate insight—into one's own inner identity, which should be the intention of one seeking to be a truly capable scientist in dealing with the kinds of issues of economy which I present here and now.

This is the quality achieved by what we should recognize in the development of the deeply self-critical mind of the greatest Classical artists and scientists. The issue is the sense of "the place" of one's personal identity, that sense of "I" which is required for compassionate insight into the same great issues which must be recognized as having shaped the potential for success or failure of great leaders such as an Abraham Lincoln or Franklin D. Roosevelt.

This quality of compassionate insight, is the hallmark of the potential for a morally great Classical artist, a great scientist, or an actually capable economist.

The Creative Identity

Speaking clinically, there are two relevant, distinctly classifiable types of creative personalities. One is creative by impulse, but does not understand exactly why this is so. This is the more typical among those cases which I have encountered, directly or indirectly. The other type, typified by such cases as Percy Bysshe Shelley for notable English thinkers, is actively self-conscious of his, or her creativity, as were true geniuses of other cultures, such as Nicholas of Cusa, Gottfried Leibniz, Gauss, Dirichlet, Riemann, and Einstein. In cases of the latter general classification, I know, personally, that their sense of personal creative identity is as-

To grasp those conceptions which are indispensable for understanding the subject of economy, LaRouche writes, "there must be a certain, definite kind of shift in the individual's sense of 'the location of' a sensed personal identity, a shift which I recognize in the work of a number of scientific minds, such as Einstein himself."

sociated with their habit of looking at their own experience of sense-perceptions which are being considered by them as attachment-like "external objects," rather than merely a sensed, shadow-like experience of their own, internal, mental-creative processes.

It is of the greatest importance in all science, that the shift away from the conception of oneself as an object of a perceived experience, to that of a self-consciously conceiving experience, is the crucial distinction of the fully conscious creative identity.[23]

It is that latter, higher order of sense of one's inner self, which is the hallmark of all actually, consciously creative intellects. A controllable access to one's own creative potential, is what is located by me, exactly, in those terms of reference. That location is associated immediately with the activity of ironical forms of Classical artistic composition, as the concluding paragraph of Shelley's **A Defence of Poetry** exemplifies this.

It is creativity as located, thus, in Classical modes of artistic composition, not physical science as usually

---

23. I cite the case of Chancellor Bismarck as illustration of that quality of distinction of the power of insight of the perceiver, from one who sees himself, or herself as merely a perceived, role-playing identity. Two instances in Bismarck's role as Chancellor are most notable. The first is his view, in practice, of the Franco-Prussian war, as distinguished from the role of Field Marshal Helmuth von Moltke. Here, Bismarck was the sanest man of rank in the situation; he understood that once the British puppet, Napoleon III was ousted, Prussia must make peace and partnership with France, in order that Britain should not be able to use France and Germany against one another. The second was Bismarck's secret agreement with Russia's Czar, that Germany would not support Austria's Habsburg in a Balkan war. For that reason, Bismarck was dumped and what became World War I was set into motion, a war which Bismarck foresaw as, in his choice of words, "a new Seven Years War." So, dumb, intrinsically incompetent U.S. commanders go to war in Afghanistan now, as evil Prime Minister Tony Blair had suckered silly President George W. Bush, Jr. into an Iraq war. As my wife, Helga Zepp-LaRouche emphasizes, most leaders of Germany, still today, will not mention the truth about Bismarck's close collaboration with the U.S.A.'s Henry C. Carey in crafting Germany's economic Bismarck reforms.

identified, which is the actual wellspring of true scientific creativity. It is from the vantage-point of Classical artistic creativity, that the knowledge of, and impetus for creativity in physical science, or economy, is derived. That suggestion of the "outsidedness" of the creative function, relative to subject-matters of experimental physical science, is the key to a competent insight into those ontological implications of the Leibniz calculus which the Eighteenth-century followers of Conti and Voltaire either failed, or simply refused to understand.

Thus, the very notion of a qualitative separation of Classical art from physical science, tends to the effect of the more or less complete destruction of all creative functions of the individual. The destruction of scientific creativity, as it has dominated the economic and artistic life of modern trans-Atlantic cultures, increasingly, since the death of President Franklin Roosevelt, is to be traced in its origins, not so much to problems within what is usually esteemed as the department of physical science, but, often, in the destruction of the creativity, and also the morality, of the actual, or nominal scientist.

It is exactly for that reason, that the promotion of the positivism of Ernst Mach and Bertrand Russell, successively, had generated the great crises of failures in the field of Twentieth-century physical science generally. The Bohm-Einstein controversy is a most appropriate kind of example of the degeneration of the talented Bohm under the influence of the positivists. The wasting of virtually entire generations of what had been, or could have been valuable contributors to fundamental scientific progress, must be traced, chiefly, to the combined effect of the impact of both Twentieth-century positivism and a scatological trend in degenerate forms of artistic life, in wrecking much of the potential for scientific and related progress among now four generations of professionals, especially the recent three.

I mean destruction as effected through that cancer of modern, anti-Classical artistic entertainments which was promoted through political undertakings such as the European Congress for Cultural Freedom and the pro-Satanic cult of that text known by the title of **The Authoritarian Personality**.

Therein, in that separation of the idea of the person from that of a temporary occupant of his human living body, a sense of separation reinforced by such perversions as those, lies the evil inherent in the current economic and social policies of President Obama and his inner circle of behaviorist advocates of those methods

of population control adopted, in September 1939, by the dictator Adolf Hitler. There lies the essence of the evil effect on a general population of a British monarchy represented by the ailing Prince Philip presently.

The stated and implicit connections represented by what I have said throughout this chapter, thus far, are best considered from the vantage-point of Vernadsky's distinction of the respective functions of the abiotic, the Biosphere, and the Noösphere. Man acts willfully upon the abiotic domain and the Biosphere, and acts upon himself, primarily, in respect to the Noösphere within which true human creativity is to be defined by us, here.

How Satan Hates Mankind

From the standpoint of as much as I presently know of the matter personally, in each relevant case, the man creates the Satan in himself. This is done, to the best of my knowledge, as a product of what Philo of Alexandria condemned as the systemic, reductionist fallacy of Aristotle's teaching. Philo accused the Aristoteleans of his time, of arguing that the power of the Creator to continue creating, ended within the completion of any initial assembly of the universe. On the contrary, authentic Christian belief regards the nature of God as that of the eternally living Creator who subsumes time itself within a simultaneity of eternity. The same view is expressed, for Judaism, by Philo. Wise rabbis teach that the Messiah will come when God decides, not according to anyone's preset time-table.

As often, a teaching, especially one conceived as a matter of *a-priorism*, is, on the one side, simply wrong in itself; but, on the other, practical side, it is wrongful in its influence as a teaching to mankind. In the case of the Aristotelean argument attacked by Philo, both effects apply. The point of the Aristotelean argument is either intended to the same, pro-Satanic effect, as the ban on man's knowledge of fire, or nuclear power, as by the Olympian Zeus of Aeschylus' **Prometheus Bound**, or, it represents the promotion of neo-Malthusian "environmentalism" by the frankly satanic Prince Philip of World Wildlife Fund notoriety, and by President Barack Obama's current retinue of behaviorist promoters of the revival now, of the current British empire's pro-genocidal 1939-1945 health-care law of Adolf Hitler, for the world of today.

Thus, on all counts, the systemic features of the current economic policies of the President Barack Obama administration, are clearly pro-Satanic. By examining what is being uttered by certain former members of our

"The wasting of virtually entire generations of what had been, or could have been valuable contributors to fundamental scientific progress, must be traced, chiefly, to the combined effect of the impact of both Twentieth-century positivism and a scatological trend in degenerate forms of artistic life. . . ." Wassily Kandinsky's "Composition VII" (1913) is typical of the type of modern art promoted by the degenerate Congress of Cultural Freedom.

legislatures and comparable other political figures, I am enabled to recognize, from the relevant footprints, exactly whence their support for Obama's current, British, pro-Satanic health-care and related social policies has been derived.

In brief, it is through such denials of the creative nature specific to mankind, that the denial of the true value of the continuation of even the most imperilled human life, as by the current policies of President Obama, is to be recognized. Any denial of that value of a human life, as was done by Adolf Hitler and his followers of today, such as Obama's Peter Orszag, is implicitly a Satanic act with the most probable consequences being a replica of the post-September 1939, Malthusian policies of the intrinsically Satanic policies of not only Adolf Hitler, then, but of Britain's Prince Philip and his toadies, such as slimy Tony Blair, today.

These are the leading implications of today's rejection, as by the "Greenies" of the world, of that power of creativity which is specific to mankind. Any economic policy, of any nation, which imperils the value of human life systemically, as the policies of President Obama's behaviorists do, must be regarded, and opposed, as purely evil, that by any actually sane and moral citizens of our republic, most emphatically. We shall not tolerate, in our own republic, what is typified by the specific, murderous swinishness of the traditional role of the British Empire in Africa still today.

However, our mission is not merely to destroy what is evilly wrong, but, rather, to affirm the beauty of the conception of the living human individual.

Shelley's Place in Man's Creativity

It is within the inner identity of the individual person, as I have located that, relative to perception, here, thus far, that the actual function of true creativity is met directly. This function is the location of the process through which the individual human mind translates mere sense-perceptions into those conceptions of the experienced world as known to the conscious mind. This is to be done, as through a means frequently identified as specifically "human insight," as by the Wolfgang Köhler associated with Max Planck. We meet what may be considered as the higher quality of function of the individual's same mental sense of identity, in what we meet as the creation of the mental images which we are to associate with the formation of those hypotheses from which discoveries of general principle, called universal principle, or even simply "ideas," are derived.

Such is the character of the cognitive functions on which our attention is being focussed here.

These functions, bearing, as they do, on the human individual's creative processes, are familiar to literate people as the touching-up of the notions of *irony* in general, and *metaphor* more emphatically.[24] These functions are associated with musicality, as adumbrated in Classical prosody, and more explicitly in the vocal, polyphonic counterpoint conceived as the legacy of Johann Sebastian Bach. Without an environment permeated with the impact of those Classical media of artistic communication, the function of creativity is not easily attained in that relevant case of a society as a whole.

The development of valid ideas, depends upon the inner voice of Classical musical-prosodic, contrapuntal modalities. The creative mind, once habituated to such creative and related activities, tends to wish to dream in color, rather than the black and white of the mere math-

---

24. Cf. William Empson, **Seven Types of Ambiguity**, for a useful reference respecting those usages.

ematician or accountant. The dream-world's anticipation of color comes from the relationship of voice-registration and polyphonic counterpoint.

The relevant expression is, that this kind of organization of the Classically developed dreaming mind, awake or sleeping, provides the basis for imparting a sense of the creative process to the conscious behavior of the individual, and the sharing of the experience of such processes among individuals.

The rhythmic experience of regular, appropriately paced, musically long walks, tends to serve as a ground-bass for the promotion of the experience of the creative process, provided that the walker is, as it is said, "up to" that specific kind of habitual self-challenge.

"Let's take a walk." The life's experience associated with the cultivation of such habits bearing upon the setting of the creative process within the individual person so acclimated, spills over as enthusiasm for expression of ideas of all sorts in the media of Classical poetry, sung musical enjoyment, and the like. Such, I must confess, all other facts considered, was the pleasing touch of seeming magic in the Hugo Wolf setting of Eduard Mörike's "Fussreise."

On the Subject of Immortality

"... At such periods, there is an accumulation of the power of receiving and imparting impassioned conceptions respecting man and nature. The persons in whom this power resides, may often, as far as regards many portions of their nature, have little apparent correspondence with that spirit of good of which they are the ministers. But, even while they deny and abjure, they are yet compelled to serve, that power which is seated on the throne of their own soul. ... it is less their spirit, than the spirit of their age."
—Percy Bysshe Shelley, 1819.

As I have already written in this report, the principle of dynamics, as introduced to modern treatments by Gottfried Leibniz, bounds the orbits of developments in society, as Kepler presents the spectacle of gravitation's regulation of the arrangement of the orbiting bodies of our Solar system.

The influences which produce the effects of dynamics in the domain of the ideas of a people which may be considered as embodying a more or less well-integrated, single social-cultural process, have an effect which resonates in the domain of the processes in which choices of opinions are shaped to form a pattern among the beliefs and actions of the members of that population.

Persons, as individuals, have within themselves the power to resist those patterns, either for good, or for evil; but, significant expressions of such resistance to patterns for evil are exceptional in respect to the ration of persons who are disposed to become a "revolutionary" of that sort. Only a relative handful of exceptional persons will ignite the spark which may ignite a new, mighty force of opinion within the body of the population considered in the relatively large.

Such is the repeated case of the impact on the culture of the German language by the collaboration of, chiefly, Gotthold Lessing and Moses Mendelssohn, and, in a related process, the spread of the musical revolution of Johann Sebastian Bach, through aid of a network of influential Jewish families of Germany and Austria who organized much of the backing for the work of Haydn, Wolfgang Mozart, Ludwig van Beethoven, Franz Schubert, and Robert and Clara Schumann, and also the circles of Johannes Brahms to the end of his life. When we add to this, the upsurge of the Nineteenth-century contributions to science and Classical culture by the Jews freed because of the influence centered on Moses Mendelssohn, continuing into the period of World War I, we have a clearer image of the reality of Shelley's view on the wide-spreading role of dynamics radiating from Classical artistic life into certain qualities of moods in the larger part of the population.

The principle which competently encompasses such a social phenomenon expresses that spark of genius on which all great movements for advancement of the human moral and scientific practice largely depend. This is the key to understanding the nature and role of artistic creativity's impact on scientific and related creativity within crucially significant strata of the society at large.

Now, focus, in that spirit and outlook, on those specific qualities of ideas which correspond, as Kepler's uniquely original discovery of a principle of universal gravitation does, to truly universal physical principles.

The characteristic of such ideas, as that case is illustrated by the echo of the discoveries by Cardinal Nicholas of Cusa, in those of Leonardo da Vinci, and the echo of the principled conceptions of Cusa and Leonardo in the original universal discovery by Kepler, provides us

Moses Mendelssohn (left) and his collaborators and followers, such as Robert and Clara Schumann, produced a cultural Renaissance in Germany in the 19th Century.

a crucially suitable example of the notion of the manner in which we encounter the expressions of immortality, as an adducible simultaneity of eternity, in the development of the process of discovery of a true universal principle as such an expression.

In such instances as that, the idea of that universal principle, transcends the mortality of the discoverers. It is the realization of the expression of such ideas, which is the true experience of history so experienced as a medium of spiritual immortality. The personality of the living human individual, when realized to such effect, is such, that for the sake of the expression of that immortality, we may defy the proscriptions of the Satanic likeness of an Olympian Zeus, by demanding principled forms of fundamental progress in the condition and powers of the human species.

Similarly, but to contrary effect, it is from this van-tage-point that we recognize the intrinsically Satanic character of the Malthusian, or so-called "Green" type of present times, or, the same quality of nature-lovers such as the Nazi Party's Hermann Göring et al., of that Party's retreats to late 1920s Summertime, countryside encampments, or Britain's Prince Philip and his son Prince Charles, or their lying protégé, former U.S. Vice-President Al Gore, now. Such are the roots of the "Green fascist" influence, sprung as if from rural Nazi retreats associated with Hermann Göring during the 1920s, whose echoes were employed by British agents to drive middle through late 1980s Germany to a virtual state of insurrectionary violence over issues of nuclear technology.

Such, for better or worse, are the types of the social processes which grip the world as a whole in these present times of existential planetary crises.

Amid all this, as some theologians might argue, "we are made mortal flesh" that we might perform the immortal mission of furthering the intrinsically anti-entropic work of continuing creation, and we might be made happy in mortal life, by the delight of being the instrument of such a lovely mission.

We may come in this way, thus, to the recognition that those ideas which are elaborated as universal principles, are not fixed ideas, but living ones, ideas which develop and evolve as human individuals and their societies are implicitly obliged, as if by the Creator, to do. So, each generation of people which is permitted or encouraged to pursue devotion to such life's work, is participating in a process of Creation.

Then, look up to the Heavens, whence the great mariners of hundreds of thousands of years ago were guided to an intended destination across even the span of oceans, even as the constellations so employed were changing in ways which needed to be discovered as keys to future destinations. Think so, of universals, over great spans of lapsed times. Think, not of events, but of long-ranging processes within a simultaneity of eternity.

Ask, then, "Who are we, that we shall have lived and died in this way? Where is mankind going, while living and dying, in such great voyages within a simultaneity of always changing eternity?" We should come to know, thus, that we live eternally as persons in such an eternity, if we live, at all, in such a choice of mission, with such a purpose in living.

Such thoughts clear the mind of cobwebs; our mission then becomes clear, and joyful. We live, on the one hand, in the flesh we inhabit, but our immortal identity dwells in our sense of our identity as a self-conceiving experience. That is to be understood as the primary, encompassing subject of an obligatory attitude of a true science of physical economy.

Now, so liberated, we are freed, as if now unencumbered, to, as it is said, get down, with resolution, to the matters immediately at hand.

Some Causes of Disaster in Europe

The essential fault of the existing constitutions of nations of European culture, other than what our Federal republic was composed to be, and to become, is that they proceed out of a notion of a form of an evolving body of "basic law," rather than a Constitution like our own. On this account, our U.S. Federal Constitution has *four principal historical characteristics*, as follows:

First, we in the future United States of today, were established as a future nation by certain colonists from Europe, whose intention was to realize the appropriate mission for European civilization's future, at a time, up to the present day, that Europe itself remains, still encumbered with many unresolved relics of an oligarchical past. *The most notable of the numerous corrupting encumbrances of Europe's history, still to date, is embedded as the intrinsically imperialist notion of monetary systems as such.* The idea of a Keynesian system, as I have identified this in earlier chapters of this present report, is the most typical of such intrinsically oligarchical encumbrances, today.

Second, that the concept of a European form of an imperial oligarchical system of political rule and social customs, suffers still from living relics of the fact that European political systems of today, had their leading essential origins in the oligarchical systems of Asia, notably the monetary systems typified into Roman imperial times, and beyond by the monetarist system centered on such principal locations as the oracle of Delphi.

The European form of an oligarchical world system not only emerged as an outgrowth of what were combined as ruinous effects of the so-called Peloponnesian War and the death of Alexander the Great. Since those developments, the imperial oligarchical systems with dominant maritime attributes, which were centered on the Mediterranean Sea until developments which occurred after the Norman Conquest, have come to dominate the entire planet as a single, extended system, which has been based, to the present day, on a monetar-

ist principle. All the systems of government dominating Europe, still today, are genetically extensions of the imperial principle known as monetarism, in sharp contrast to the constitutional credit-system of our U.S.A.

Third, European parliamentary systems are essentially relics of feudalism. The presence of oligarchical classes of families and persons, and the substitution of merely general law of the state-system, or its like, for the subsuming authority of a Constitution conceived in natural law and defined by its self-assigned mission, represents a deep cleavage in matter of principle from the notion of the mission-oriented, constitutional commitment to destiny of the true American System of political-economy.

Fourth, the resurgence of the feudalist imperial principle called "globalization," is an expression of the innate disposition of European systems for a return to what is perceived, ideologically, as a natural expression of a still underlying notion of the Eurasian utopianism which is never far from Babylon and from the Achaemenid empire's imperialism, which is close to the surface of the passions, inherited from the evil of the underlying British imperial ideological influence, among European nations generally, still today. The British imperial thrust for overthrowing the 1648 Treaty of Westphalia, is a clear demonstration of such European tendencies toward reverting to medieval and even uglier forms of traditional moral depravities.

During the span, from ancient to present times, there have been some exceptions to the depraved tendencies embedded in ancient European and other oligarchical forms of traditions, of which the most notable has been the emergence of our United States, within its development realized under President Abraham Lincoln's steps toward fulfillment of former Secretary of State John Quincy Adams' intention, as celebrated in 1876, of a single continental republic, from the Atlantic to the Pacific and between its Canadian and Mexican borders.

However, the U.S.A., which had a leading role for a time, especially under President Franklin Roosevelt's leadership, had never actually replaced entirely the global imperialist, monetarism-based system, which has been a moral disease whose influence has been chiefly exerted from, and centered within our republic's, and civilization's chief and chronic adversary, the United Kingdom of England, Scotland, and Wales.

From early in its beginnings, in our English-speaking settlement in North America, as in New England between 1620 and 1688, and under the emerging role of Benjamin Franklin later, especially after the establishment of the British East India Company as a private empire under Lord Shelburne's direction through the February 1763 Peace of Paris, until the English treaty-negotiations set into motion under the newly created British Foreign Office in 1782, the cause of the freedom of what was to become the United States remained a crucial factor of change in the political life of globally extended European developments.

The 1776 U.S. Declaration of Independence, Alexander Hamilton's role in defining the design of the U.S. credit system and its associated national banking system, and the adoption of the Preamble of the U.S. Federal Constitution, were each, and all the crucial markers in a process which established the Federal Republic of the United States as the only true republic of our planet, and the only nation constitutionally free of the corruption of an imperial international monetary system, an imperial system in fact, controlled, to the present day, by the Venetian financier power of the so-called Liberalism of Paolo Sarpi and his followers. That latter, financier cabal, with the whimpering sophistries of other European states taken into account, is the reality of the reign of British imperialism over Europe, Africa, and beyond, still today.

Many Europeans would dispute this characterization, but that denial is an all the more pitiable sophistry, by means of which many continental Europeans have sought as to deny the obvious truth respecting their own actual, still afflicted conditions of government. The most nearly comparable case of sheer silliness, is that of a current within the U.S.A. which has sometimes admired itself for that faction's adopted image of the U.S.A. as a supposed leading world power over a succession of decades during which, no Presidency or session of the Congress has actually defied the power of British imperialism, since the new round of changes dooming the Bretton Woods agreements, which were imposed upon the U.S.A. of March 1, 1968.

Admittedly, there are pockets of resistance to this world-spanning British Empire even now. Nonetheless, the only current trend which menaces the march toward a single, world-wide British Empire, an empire under the constitution of a new, globalist Tower of Babel, is the greater probability, that the entire world economy is now at the verge of simply disintegrating into an ungovernable, planetary new dark age of ungovernable, genocidal chaos.

Where We Have Arrived Today

Since the awful betrayal of principle which occurred in our U.S.A. on April 13, 1945, there has been a long wave of erosion of the potential for an improvement of the long-term prospects of the world as a whole. That is to emphasize that short- to medium-term changes in apparent trends are not always moving in the apparent same direction as the more decisive, long-term trends in the more decisive factor of physical-capital formation.

The fact of such self-contradictory trends and patterns, suffices, in itself, to prompt intelligent observers to rely on the application of that principle of *dynamics* introduced by Gottfried Leibniz in 1695, or, the Riemannian successor of elementary dynamics, the conception of the Gauss-Riemannian tensor associated, most notably, with the influence of Albert Einstein and Academician V.I. Vernadsky.

The simpler form of approximation of this role of the tensor concept, is representable by conceiving of a function, in which the estimable, accumulated remaining life of the usefulness of existing physical capital investment in essential physical capital of combined infrastructure and production, is compared with the rate of changes in direction and quality of that net capital stock as examined in per-capita and per-square-kilometer terms.[25]

Estimates of that sort for net of cumulative investments, must be supplemented with consideration of forms of depletion, including of the relative best quality of so-called natural resources, and the effects, expressed in accelerated depreciation prompted by depletion of best resources, of factors of relative technological obsolescence, economic effects of decadence of popular culture on productivity, as in the U.S.A. since April 1945, and so on.

These considerations which are notable as in the form of or near to physical-capital factors, must be supplemented by anticipation of the physical-economic losses caused by a decadent swing against creativity and morals of the type associated with the influence of the European Congress for Cultural Freedom and the greatly damaging intellectual and moral effects of **The Authoritarian Personality** of Theodor Adorno et al.

On the opposing side, we have the beneficial effects of an upturn in the influence of truly Classical culture, better qualities of education, and the like.

---

25. My "Triple Curve" functions are a form of pedagogical reflection of such considerations.

For example, there has been a net contraction in the useful investments in basic economic physical infrastructure of the U.S.A. since Fiscal Year 1967-1968, and a related cutback in capital and related expenditures for investment in development of new advanced technologies since about time.

Soon, then, already during the early through middle 1970s, the U.S. would reach the point that we were losing the very same technologies, as if drip by drip, which had been represented with each progress in the implementation of the space program. This pattern, occurred under the associated condition, that the gains in technology resulting from the space program's development were estimated at near to ten times the cost of those developments! From the election of President Richard Nixon on, the trends in U.S. technology, measured per capita and per square kilometer, have been declining at an accelerating rate, with the greatest rate of decline occurring through the recently accelerating influence of so-called "globalization."

This has now reached the point, that the losses attributable to shift of production from the U.S.A., to China, have led to irreparable losses in the export market for the Chinese goods on which the stability of China's economy had depended, with no hope of an adequate recovery for China in sight, whereas the U.S. economy itself is now plunging into some deep pit, under the new, Obama administration, that at an accelerating rate.

In the meantime, since July 2007, neither the U.S. economy nor any of Europe have managed to do anything right!

The Decline of the Individual Mind

Some decades now past, I presented a fabulous picture of the direction in which developments in the U.S. economy were already proceeding. I painted a word-picture of a magnificent skyscraper, implicitly in Detroit, Michigan, in which the fabled world-wide industrial might of the U.S.A., had, at last, been successfully concentrated. It was said that the only fault in this wondrous work of Wall Street's perfection, was that the entire industry of the nation was concentrated in one little old man, nearing retirement, although still, for the time being, pounding out product with a hammer, in the basement.

NASA

Already, during the 1970s, the U.S. was losing the spectacular advances in technology developed for the space program. Since then, the U.S. has been declining, with the greatest rate of decline during the recent era of globalization. Shown, Apollo 17 astronaut Jack Schmitt on the Moon, with the Earth above, Dec. 11, 1972: the final manned Moon mission.

With that, the legendary Paradise of the "new Malthusians" had nearly arrived.

Among other bad news of the moment, throughout this planet, the present government of the United States is, at this present moment, temporarily, or otherwise, utterly, clinically insane, and probably, on the basis of reading of President Obama's statements of intent, as much given to celebrate mass murder, perhaps at places such as Green Bay, Wisconsin, as the Roman Emperor Nero, to boot. A man who might brag about the death of his grandmother, perhaps because his mother was not available for mention at the time, who is likely to do such things, perhaps out of envy against Nero, and, who might choose to make as much as three tries at murdering his most trusted advisor, before succeeding in a fourth attempt, is not my recommended choice for an heroic model of timely leadership, or, even to be made the head of the local lodge.[26]

---

26. Perhaps you dislike my rudeness toward a figure who is yet to perpetrate his greatest crimes. Perhaps you have not yet understood Boc-

IV. A Global Credit-System

*That much said thus far, and much more could be said to kindred effect, let us now, so prepared by our intervening discussion here, return to the notion which I expressed in the preceding chapter, as **"The shift away from the conception of oneself as an object of a perceived experience, to that of a self-consciously conceiving experience . . . the crucial distinction of the fully conscious, creative identity."**[27]*

It is relevant, and necessary, to open this chapter of my report, by emphasizing that, on performance, I have been repeatedly the most successful economic forecaster of the consequences of long-range of trends in economic policy, during longer than a quarter-century, including my now crucial, fully vindicated forecast in an international webcast, of the presently continued global breakdown-crisis, which I presented on July 25, 2007.

However, I am not a pessimist, neither by conviction, nor in temperament. Nevertheless, at the present moment, the unavoidable fact is, that in the view of anyone thinking competently about the ABCs of economy, the prospect for the survival of the present world system of nation-state economies, is very much in doubt. I make no prediction that the human species is going to cease to exist in the biological form which we might easily recognize today; but, at this point, unless the present course of the U.S. Barack Obama government is sharply reversed, it is now a scientific fact, that, already, during its remaining early days, as is shown from the direction which the Obama government has taken, since the recent visits to Washington, D.C. of both Britain's Prime Minister Brown and that Minister's virtual mortal adversary, former Prime Minister Blair, there is not going to be what can be recognized,

Creative Commons/Downing Street

Unless the present course of the Obama regime is sharply reversed, away from the direction it has taken since the visits of Britain's Gordon Brown and Tony Blair, LaRouche warns, "there is not going to be what can be recognized, much longer, as our constitutional system of government."

much longer, as either our constitutional system of government, or as a decent standard of welfare for our own citizens and their progeny, unless the present Obama health-care policy is summarily, and completely dumped.

Given those present policies, launched under the former U.S. Presidency of George W. Bush, Jr, and continued, and aggravated under President Obama thus far, and under the set of presently leading conditions in progress in our republic, and also world-wide, now, the population of all nations of the world will be greatly reduced at a rapid rate, and there will be nothing like the present semblance of national government in any part of the world. In that case, we might expect population levels to reach late Fourteenth Century levels of death-rates, or, even worse, and we should foresee even the possible vanishing of entire nations, and also language-cultures, at various points during the course of even the presently oncoming next generation.

However, the irony of the present world situation is, that, even at this late stage, there is no *necessary* reason that the present drift toward global Hell could not be reversed along lines which I am confident should be, or might be adopted, were the right people to come to their senses soon. However, any such happier outcome for

---

caccio's **Decameron**, Rabelais' **Pantagruel**, or Cervantes' ridicule of a Habsburg tyrant. The true prophets from evil times, reduce ogres to their true size, as ordinary men and women, as if to unmask the silliness of what fools had feared as the mighty Wizard of Oz, that the would-be monster might be treated on more appropriate terms.

27. *supra.* p. 33.

the better, for any part of the world, today, would seem to be, at the present moment, an almost unbelievable miracle, if our visions continue to be limited to viewing matters from the standpoint of the behavior of certain leading people of leading nations, including our own, right now.

That said, let us agree, nonetheless, here and now, to examine the best alternatives available to our planet now, looking at the present U.S. and world situation within the range of what my expertise as a successful forecaster tells me is actually possible now.

"Yes, Myrtle, there is no good reason that we could not, now, begin a general process of national and also global physical-economic recovery," a recovery to be measured in per capita and per square kilometer terms. This could happen, if some people in the right positions, were willing to make the sudden, rather radical changes, which could send our nation, and also this planet, into the kind of a turnabout which brings the world at large into an initially slow start toward economic recovery, and which leads into what must become an accelerating general recovery, toward far better than "status-quo-ante" conditions and trends.

Therefore, I report that I am optimistic on that point, but, I warn that I have grave doubts, as the venerable Quaker said, "about thee," about most among the rest of you in leading positions of policy-shaping, world-wide, now. Remedies exist, but only on the condition that they enjoy timely and energetic support. The "other guy" on whom you are relying to bring forth the needed changes in policy, is probably not going to do the job. You must.

Therefore, to begin this part of our report, let us speak here as little as possible about the subject of money itself. Nonetheless, we can and must say, simply, that if the U.S. Government takes the actions which I have already prescribed, there will be enough money, in large part, in good banks for what is absolutely necessary to be done in support of the recovery-process.

That means, that by adopting a Glass-Steagall measuring rod, and returning to a pre-Nixon Administration practice of Hill-Burton health-care policy for the nation, all combined with a switch, back to a global fixed-exchange-rate system (through reorganization in Federally supervised bankruptcy), and if we replace the world's hopelessly bankrupt monetary systems, by an anti-Keynesian, Hamiltonian form of credit system, that of the type which President Franklin Roosevelt had prepared and intended for the post-war world, we would be able to work our way back to recovery, beginning now.

A lot of "ifs," but that, nonetheless, is the world's situation as we have it, now.

"Impossible!" some might cry! Not at all. When even folk like that are scared enough, and they are, presently, about to be very, very frightened by developments already in the pipelines, they—at least the sane ones—are going to begin to say: "Tell me again that thing you and I were talking about; maybe it deserves a second hearing."

"What about my money!" will be one of the first questions they will raise, then.

Let us get that issue of "my money" quickly out of the way, first, so that it does not continue to block our attention to the actions through which we, here and in places abroad, must work out certain very important agreements.

Let Us Review That Situation, Briefly

Before getting into the scientific meat of the present world situation, let us speak of the continuation of recent trends, as follows. That situation is the following.

On July 25, 2007, I delivered a certain international webcast, during which I warned, that the world, including our U.S.A., was on the verge of a general breakdown-crisis which would begin with a financial collapse at the weakest point in the world's then existing financial system, a bloated real-estate mortgage market which was already more than overripe to blow almost immediately.

Within seventy-two hours, the first such blow against which I had just warned days earlier, struck. Swindlers and fools, alike, called it "a sub-prime mortgage crisis." (What a collection of liars and dupes!) It was the beginning of what soon showed itself to be, a chain-reaction sort of blow-out of the entire world financial system, as anyone in leading positions in the world, who is not virtually brain-dead, or off getting a belly-button-lint check-up somewhere in the Himalayas, should recognize as fact, by now.

I made some urgently needed, initial recommendations for immediate action, during that same webcast. My first concern, was to save what used to be the Glass-Steagall category of the nation's regular banking system. That means: not the Monopoly-game-like, imaginary money, uttered by places such as Wall Street, but the part of the chartered banking system on which economic life in states and local communities depends, if we are to keep the relevant regions' physical economy operating. That meant that the great mass of gambling debts, such as the financial derivatives hoax, would be scrapped; only legitimate, regular, national and state chartered banks, on which we rely to service the economy of the state and local communities, could, and would be supported.

After all, Wall Street's plunge into bankruptcies, had all occurred as a result of its own foolish initiatives. Moreover, most of that paper which went down in the great Wall Street crash of the past year (and was, foolishly, bailed out), was essentially toy money, of that type called financial derivatives. It is those swindlers, world-wide, who had made the mistake; it was they who should have taken the heat for the swindle which they themselves had created; and, it was they who should bear the full burden, still now, of the penalties which they have actually earned, as all bad laws lately adopted must also be annulled now.

This meant, that, back in July 2007, and later, that I was prescribing a rescue of the most essential, legitimate economic interests of the government and ordinary people of the United Sates, all of which is broadly similar to the way President Franklin Roosevelt had led the rescue of our imperilled national economy during his first days in office, and later, too. Roosevelt had succeeded then; we could succeed now.

I had proposed some other, matching specific measures, all of which I had made public by mid-September of 2007.

All that I had proposed, then, would have worked as I had intended; but, our government, including key members of the U.S. Congress, deployed like grave-robbers, as if to steal everything in sight, all for the intended benefit, not of our nation, but for the advantage of the swindlers with whom some members of the Federal U.S. Congress and other parts of our Federal Government were "in cahoots." So, the problem has been, that some people, including leading members of the Congress, let the Wall Street hogs loose to eat the chickens. Since that time, it has not been the bulls or bears of Wall Street, but the hogs of the London-centered financial world, which have looted every nation

LaRouche's proposals for rescuing our economy would have worked—but, "our government, including key members of the U.S. Congress, deployed like grave-robbers to steal everything in sight, all for the intended benefit, not of our nation, but for the advantage of the swindlers" with whom, some were "in cahoots." Shown: Nancy Pelosi, with her partners in crime.

of the world, including our U. S. Government, and also your personal health-care resources, as President Obama himself is doing right now. This course of action was taken, all to bail out the biggest, and most useless pack of financial swindlers throughout the world today, a pack of creatures of an incarnate depravity, the like of which today's world probably could not remember that it had seen before. That left very little financial support available for stabilizing the part of the economy in which our ordinary citizens live, including our capacity to produce the real wealth on which our republic depends for its continued existence, for the production on which our people depend, and to provide the employment and other essentials of daily personal and community life.

So, the recently elected President Obama had joined ranks with the grave robbers, until now. I continue to wish and hope that he would improve. However, if he does not change, or we do not get him under control, and turn him around, very soon, this nation of ours is about to go down the shaft to a certain kind of Hell, soon. We are, for example, presently operating within a range of about a month or so, perhaps less, before the already growing impossibility of avoiding a chain-reaction collapse of the economy of the entire planet starts to kick in.

So, if there is no sudden change, away from President Obama's present support for what are the actually insane and mass-murderous health-care and other economic policies which the Obama administration has imported from London, there is virtually no chance that either our republic, or the rest of the world, either, is not going to plunge into a global breakdown-crisis more awful than what was known as Europe's Fourteenth-century "New Dark Age."

Under these circumstances, only a fool would complain that I am refusing to accept that President's current economic and health-care policies.

Remember! Back then, during Europe's awful Fourteenth-century breakdown crisis, a crisis all too similar to the world's own breaking out at this present time, about half the communities of Europe ceased to exist, and about one-third of the population disappeared. The prospect for the world, right now, is far worse, unless we make the necessary return to the tradition of our President Franklin D. Roosevelt, now.

However, that said, there is nothing actually inevitable in the continuation of this present oncoming, global, economic breakdown-crisis. It is not a natural crisis. It is entirely a result of the wrong kinds of people being in the right high places. So, you could say, all considered, rather fairly, I think, that, in the meantime, some people in leading positions, including some in our U.S. Congress, have done something tantamount to each talking their own head and rear end into switching places. In other words, very little is happening which could not be repaired, if the right people, with the right policies, were placed in charge.

Putting the right people in charge quickly enough, is difficult, but it can be done. Getting the right policies, is difficult, but the real problem is that there are very few people who are now trained even to know what to do about the crucial problem, even people within the very top layer of the presently ongoing international negotiations. That top-ranking layer is that which must be moved, or removed, if the world is to adopt that which must be adopted, if we are to come out of what is already the presently onrushing world economic breakdown-crisis.

Where I Come In

Designing that urgently needed rescue-policy, is where I come in. It is unfortunate, that, otherwise, there are very few persons presently entrenched in highly influential places, from around the world, who command relevant competence in these matters of design of the presently, urgently needed reform in policies.

Admittedly, I am, at the present moment of writing, a few weeks shy of eighty-seven, but I have some good years still left in me, even if I am a bit slower of foot than I once was; but, nonetheless, I still represent the rare kind of knowledge, experience, and related personal capabilities needed, to guide the right people in high places throughout the world, in dealing with the most critical part of what needs to be known, if we are to bring the presently onrushing world breakdown-crisis back under control.

The pre-eminent topic of discussion in this present chapter, will be the subject of the workings of a modern economy from the viewpoint of a science of physical economy, rather than that of a monetary system. Monetary systems exist, and the matter of the prices denominated under such a system has calculable effects, of course; but, all of the crucial matters of an economy involve physical values, not monetary ones. The fact that only a few among those carrying the title of "economist" today, have any effective comprehension of these distinctions, does not make those distinctions of mine less important, but, directly the contrary. As it is also said in respect to other kinds of professions, it is what one does not know, which is likely to hurt him, and also his neighbors, the most. That, certainly, identifies the essence of the way in which both our United States and many other parts of the world have dragged all of the world, now, into what is already the biggest and baddest general economic breakdown-crisis in the presently recorded history of the world.

It is all coming down right now.

I repeat, and insist, that there are remedies for this oncoming economic breakdown, and some aspects of this do require attention to effects of the role of money in the process. However, all of the root causes of this crisis, and also the potential cures, are physical, rather than monetary. Here, I shall touch on money when that subject is relevant, and avoid that subject as much as is possible, otherwise.

If the Dollar Goes

At the present moment, there is a scheme cooked up in British circles, to bring down the entire present world system, by pushing the present government of Russia to, in turn, push the present government of China to "dump the dollar," and to join with certain leading circles in Brazil in sinking the entire world economy, chain-reaction fashion. Such an action, by causing a sudden, deep devaluation of the U.S. dollar, would, as a simple matter of fact, cause a rather immediate, chain-reaction collapse of every monetary system of the world.

The intention of the relevant British-centered circles, is to use the event of a general breakdown of precisely all principal, present currencies of the world, as the occasion to launch a new monetary system, based on the assets presently claimed by an assortment of certain predatory, private financial organizations. The objective in sight by those predators, is the establishment of what must be described, in effect, as a new "Tower of Babel. "

That is the scheme, called "globalization," which has been the long-standing, ultimate intent of circles only typified by former British Prime Minster Tony Blair. This would be a development which would serve as the occasion for bringing down the level of the current population of the world, from the present vicinity of 6.5 billions persons, to that of about two, or less, that very rapidly.

Clearly, such a scheme would be about as therapeutic as using cyanide for the improvement of the smell of one's breath. The scheme would be a catastrophe in its own right; but what most concerns me here, is the fact that if that course of action were permitted, it would exclude the possibility of a recovery of humanity for a rather long period to come.

In other words, that "New Tower of Babel" scheme, called "globalization," would be, at its least worst, a replay of that which the medieval Venetian oligarchs did, using the Lombard bankers as tools, fools, and collateral victims, to reduce the population of Europe by an estimated one-third, back then. Speak of that British Royal Consort, a visibly dried-out Prince Philip, and his pro-genocidal "wet dream;" which is to speak of his proposal for the use of such means as the spread of deadly infectious disease to bring the present world's population down, from the vicinity of about 6.5 billions, to the vicinity of 2 billions, or less, as virtually the same proposal had been made, by the late Bertrand Russell, in 1951. The present health policy of the U.S. Obama plan for genocide against a large chunk of the current U.S. population, through a so-called "health-care reform," would be just the frosting on the evil Prince Philip's, and Bertrand Russell's genocidal cake.

On the other hand, if the U.S. government were to come to its senses, there is a quite different outcome. If the U.S.A. were joined in its effort by a set of nations including Russia, China, and India, that combination could be the basis for initiating a new, chartered credit-system, to replace the world's present monetary system. It would be a credit-system operating for the benefit of the nations of the planet as a whole, as a fixed-exchange-rate system among the respective, sovereign treaty-partners and their respective, sovereign credit-systems. Of necessity, the initial treaty-agreements would cover, minimally, a fifty-year period of initial operations.

A New World System

The immediate outcome of the needed general reform, away from neo-Malthusian horrors, would be a new design for a world system of what will be, respectively, perfectly sovereign nation-states, a system premised on the notion of the natural consequence of an extension of the 1648 Peace of Westphalia. This would be, as the Peace of Westphalia has already implied, a principled arrangement premised on the fact of a fundamental difference of existential principle between beasts, such as those allied with Britain's Tony Blair, and real people. It would represent the perfect paradigm of universal moral law for the benefit of mankind.

The model to be referenced for launching the building of a system of nation-state economies premised upon that principle, has been provided by the precedent of a successful remedy, devised by the United States' Alexander Hamilton, later the first Secretary of the Treasury of the then new American republic. The essential, principled economic consequence of that design, was the constitutional principle, that no currency of the United States can be uttered, except as part of a credit-system, rather than a monetary system, that under the constitutional authorization granted to the U.S. President by the U.S. Congress, the lower house most notably.

This constitutional principle of a credit system, was also used by then Secretary Hamilton to craft a national bank. Later, the U.S. government created a Second National Bank, to resume the custom of the lapsed First National Bank. The crucial feature of all aspects of this set of arrangements, is that the debt of the United States, so uttered, excludes control of the credit of the United

States by foreign powers, except as the U.S.A. has consented to this through lawful forms of treaty-agreements.

However, *since the Constitution of the U.S.A., unlike the constitutions of Europe, is premised on that constitutional uttering of principles of humanity's natural law, as natural law is exemplified by the work of Nicholas of Cusa and Gottfried Leibniz, rather than upon agreements such as contracts, no treaty agreement adopted by the United States modifies the essential principle of the Constitution of our United States itself.*[28]

The crucial feature of the sovereign arrangements underlying that U.S. Constitution, is that such instruments of policy defy the efforts of foreign powers, either as nations, or as private consorts, to practice usury against a sovereign republic, or its targetted citizens, as by the Obama Administration now; this needed remedy is supplied by outlawing corrupting present arrangements. On the other hand, the existence of an agreement to a relevant form of treaty-agreement among sovereign nations, will create a closed network constituting an alternative to a monetarist system. That is to be accomplished by aid of establishing a fixed-exchange agreement among the treaty partners, a treaty agreement operating as a fixed-exchange system of the type which resists the assault on the nation-partners by alien usurers.

The functioning of such a type of sovereign credit-system, also serves as the mode for uttering currency, as was employed by the United States, in the mode of "green-backs." It should be noted, on this account, that past attempts to ban "greenbacks" have been not only contrary to our Constitution, but such bans have been implicitly treasonous concoctions inserted into our republic by the subversive influence of foreign, and usually hostile powers.

---

28. This concept of "natural law," such as what is expressed by the 1648 Peace of Westphalia, or, its nearest precedent, Nicholas of Cusa's **De Pace Fidei**, does not exist under that system of British Liberalism which is typified by such followers of Paolo Sarpi as the British empire's Lord Shelburne, Adam Smith, and Jeremy Bentham. The intrinsic imperialism of Anglo-Dutch Liberalism derived from Sarpi's Ockhamite cult, implies a system of precedents situated within what is axiomatically a system of financier-oligarchical traditions of mercenary, contract law. Thus, there is no existence of actual morality among the followers of British Liberalism, or kindred sophistries respecting human nature. U.S. constitutional law is expressed in the 1776 Declaration of Independence and the statement of fundamental principle of law in the explicitly anti-Locke Preamble of U.S. Federal Constitution.

A Third National Bank

The time has now come to launch a Third National Bank of our United States, as this is to be crafted by aid of reference to the First and Second.

To illustrate that intention, this means a reorganization of the present U.S. dollar, which will be accomplished by a measure of reorganization in bankruptcy. Such a reorganization would be premised on the movement of the assets which are to be maintained in value as the equivalent amount denominated in the terms of a credit-system, rather than the relics of a doomed and virtually dead monetary system which linger in a limbo of virtual reorganization in bankruptcy. This action is premised on those relevant provisions of the U.S. Federal Constitution respecting the uttering of credit employed for the creation of lawful U.S. currency.

This correction is also to be made in recognition of the proof of constitutional principle, which has been demonstrated by the most compelling evidence to the effect, that the termination of the Glass-Steagall act which occurred at the prompting of such scoundrels as Larry Summers, is to be seen as implicitly an unconstitutional action.

That is the judgment to be made, when that action by the notoriously predatory Summers et al., is considered in the light of the implications of the experience of the U.S. in launching and implementing the Glass-Steagall law, and, also, in respect to the unconstitutional effects of the cancellation of that protection to the nation and its citizens which must have been regarded from experience as not merely enacted statute, but also implicitly constitutional rights, a latter quality which had been demonstrated to be that, in fact, by what Summers' role had shown to be the recurrence of the very kinds of evil consequences of both the situation prompting the original action during the 1930s, and shown by those recent consequences unloosed by the constitutionally wrongful repeal of that law. This repeal was shown to be in clearly intentional violation of the very foundation of the intention of our Federal Constitution's Preamble, and the earlier right to the pursuit of happiness presented in the 1776 Declaration of Independence.

There is no properly lawful statute, or custom of practice, under the original intent of our Constitutional system of government, which can be permitted to defy those essential principles of both the Declaration of Independence and the subsuming statement of constitutional intention expressed as the anti-John Locke Preamble of the Federal Constitution. Any judicial or

LaRouche calls for the establishment of a Hamiltonian Third National Bank of the United States, at this time, to address the present, global, economic-breakdown crisis. Shown, the First National Bank in Philadelphia, and, Alexander Hamilton's statue standing before the Treasury Building in Washington.

legislative rule which stands in violation of those underlying intentions expressed as the creation of our republic, is, as an elementary matter of fact, a violation, and even a betrayal of our system of constitutional law.

The urgent need for the launching of a Third National Bank of the United States, at this time, is forced upon our urgent considerations, now, by the very nature of the present, global, economic-breakdown crisis. All considerations bearing upon the urgency of certain such improvements in our system of law, are prompted, and conditioned, chiefly, both by the suffering of our own people and by our desire for good relations with other peoples, a reform which is to be promoted as the relevant, urgently needed cessation of abuses.

The implicit bankruptcy of the institutions associated with an originally misconceived, and, currently, greatly mismanaged Federal Reserve System, together, is to be compared, for its wicked effect, with the effect of the recently degenerated condition of the International Monetary Fund (IMF). The fact is that the IMF has been transmogrified, away from its original intent, into a global pestilence, and, therefore, requires both the urgent change from an international monetary system to a multi-national international system of credit, and, also, the absorbing of the assets of the im-

plicitly bankrupted Federal Reserve System into the functions of the national credit-system of a Third National Bank.

As Alexander Hamilton addressed the sorry, war-depleted condition of the banks which had been established as chartered banks by each among the earlier British colonies, so we must create an instrument of protection, combined with needed measures of reorganization in bankruptcy for those portions of the present U.S. banking system which conform to Glass-Steagall criteria. A Third National Bank would be the most appropriate instrument consistent within the framework provided implicitly by our Federal Constitution.

The included object of this reform which I have proposed, is to create the sovereign mechanisms within our own republic, under which we can launch an immediate forty-to-fifty-year program of national reconstruction of the physical economy of the United States, and also engage in relevant forms of long-term partnership in mutual benefits shared among willing and cooperating sovereign governments of other nations.

So, in the illustrative case of such a network-agreement among the U.S.A., Russia, China, and India, among others, we must foresee the creation of the long-term credit needed for investments, especially public investments, in a nation's needed development of its essential basic economic infrastructure. The range of mean life-spans of specific investments will average within a range of a half-century.

The matter of principle which is to be emphasized here, in this connection, instructs us to the following effect.

This international reform contributed by aid of the initiatives of the U.S.A. government, would put the U.S. dollar-system through reorganization in bankruptcy, using the intention embodied in the former Glass-Steagall standard, for bringing forth a set of protected, functioning chartered banks, for a newly organized, internationally fixed-exchange-rate U.S. dollar. This international system must be, however, one now premised on the same U.S. Constitutional requirement implied in the replacing of a monetary system, by a credit system of the type specified as law, as in the U.S. Federal Constitution's provisions respecting the uttering of credit as a debt of our United States.

That action would take the policy of the U.S.A. back to the hours before President Franklin Roosevelt had died.

That action requires a clearing of the head of certain most relevant, presently habituated delusions among many of our citizens, respecting the principles of economy. This must be done here, to clear the way for presenting, still later in this present chapter, the needed new views of policy-shaping on which a durable economic recovery now depends.

Adam and the Eve of Destruction

Adam Smith, that is.

That much said, I now turn to the subject of the system of national physical economy. For this purpose, I refer your attention to those earlier pages of this report in which our attention was focused upon the implications of the design of that modern form of an operating physical economy, which are implicit in the interconnected work of Bernard Riemann, Albert Einstein, and Academician V.I. Vernadsky. I begin this section, returning to my theme, that *all economic values are essentially physical, that in terms of reference to those great, modern scientific thinkers, not monetary systems.*

As I shall show from this point of reference, no notions of economic values can be presented competently in what have become the conventional terms of financial accounting and related practice,

For example: any reflective and competent management consultant, who has had sufficiently broad experience among various enterprises, could recall that the most frequent causes of failures of performance by what had been successful enterprises, are usually located in the effects of that tendency for mismanagement among those corporate financial officers and similarly relevant officials who have been misled into premising their judgments all too often on the mistaken assumption, that accounting reports are competent representations of the process for which the management of the enterprise is responsible.

It was commonplace, in my experience, that the most serious of the systemic problems of a mature enterprise for which management consultants have been called in, involved actual problems which the client's management had refused to consider as being sources of relevant problems. In the majority of such cases, especially in organizations under Wall Street-related domination, it was the influence of what was, from the standpoint of economics, that intrinsic incompetence of the accounting profession's practices which lay in assuming that accounting practice had something to do, functionally, with the principles of economy.

Thus, typical systemic problems developed more readily in those areas overlooked for reason of a management's failure to take into account, either an intrinsically misleading effect of customary financial practice itself, or an influential financial officer's misguided presumption, that areas of problems which did not lie formally within the bounds of financial accounting practice, did not exist. The case of that great price-swindle of automobile marketing practice during the 1953-1957 interval, which triggered the relatively deep 1957-58 recession, is a stellar example of this.

So, as in that case, the tendency of the accounting office to seek to dominate policy-shaping of the enterprise, as by claimed expertise in the art of crafting a report of an apparent profit, or sinking the targeted section of the operating management by reporting a disaster, was often the actual root of specific tendencies for mismanagement.

As in the matter of the 1957-1958 U.S. recession, the worst problems tended to be caused by Wall Street-controlled enterprises, as by the management of the pace-setting voice of Wall Street's General Motors interests, as distinct from what were relatively more closely held firms. The closely held firm tended to know its business; the public corporation tended toward placing the priority on Wall Street's business. From my knowledgeable examination of some of the leading consulting firms' reports to their clients, those consulting firms which were oriented to Wall Street's pleasure in speculative financial gains, tended to deliver the relatively worst performance for their clients, for reason of a primary interest of the consulting firm's own position in the financial market generally.[29]

As I am emphasizing within the course of this present chapter, the cardinal issue in management of the economy, lies in the factor of science-driven progress, an aspect of the process in which the standard practice of accounting and related financial management shows little, to no competent interest in those areas in which the battle against attrition, and for scientific and technological progress should have been at a premium. Really impressive successes in results, are usually to be traced

---

29. This is not to mention the evils associated with the special interests of the heirs of the active founders of what had been a more closely held enterprise.

to other than customary practice of innovation, especially scientific-technological innovation, or insight into market, or technological factors lying outside the firm's established assumptions concerning its corporate or related mission.

So, often in the case of a firm which had passed from a long-term profit-making, to the follies of a short-term profit-taking phase of its existence, a needed technological advance within the economy required going outside and around the problem of stubborn clinging to old, so-called "traditional" assumptions, by creating a new firm, as if from the ground up.

The general principles underlying that area of policy-shaping, were presented implicitly to the reader in earlier chapters of this report, where I emphasized the significance of the work of the poet Shelley as key to understanding the origin of the impetus for fundamental human scientific creativity, as lying within the domain of Classical artistic creativity.

At this point in this report, I shall now apply those qualifying considerations to the needed comprehension of the ongoing process of internal evolution which is the dynamic process of any economy when considered in terms of a science of physical economy.

This connection will be elaborated in the concluding sections of this present report, with a view to demystifying those real subject-matters which had been ordinarily addressed in a corrupted way, addressed from the vantage-point of those misleading, modern monetary systems whose performance has been misshaped by the influence of the role of an aspect of global maritime and monetary power which is expressed, typically, by the British Empire's dominant role in the philosophically Liberal interpretation of world economy over, most of the span of the 1763-2009 interval to date, but, more emphatically since the assassination of the President John F. Kennedy who had fought those "steel bosses" who were oriented to shut down their part of the economy.

However, to identify a common root of related problems, let us begin with some clarifying, clinical reference to the roles of the physiocrats François Quesnay and A.R.J. Turgot, roles which must be considered here as a matter of pin-pointing the psychological depravity at the root of the popularity of the evil, habitually ruinous economic dogma of Lord Shelburne's Adam Smith.

Smith's Systemic Incompetence

Although Smith's 1776, specifically anti-American **Wealth of Nations,** was largely the by-product of Smith's rapacious plundering of the then manuscripts-

in-progress of the French Physiocrat A.R.J. Turgot; the most significant writing by Smith was his earlier, 1759, **The Theory of Moral Sentiments**, in which we also meet those underlying psychological assumptions of the fascist dogma common to the behavioral economics of the putative authors of the depraved and ruinous present, behaviorist policies of President Obama.

That relatively earlier, 1759 publication by Smith, not **The Wealth of Nations**, is the most pertinent for understanding the origins, in Smith, of, specifically, the Hitler-copied health-care policy which has been dictated to President Barack Obama, thus far, from London, by the combination of the British NICE and through the vehicle of such associates of President Obama himself as Dr. Ezekiel Emanuel, Peter Orszag, et al. Those typify the set of the practices of such implicitly pro-Nazi ideologues inside the U.S. itself, which has been influencing the President's brutishly immoral health-care policies, as that same outlook is expressed in President Obama's adoption of what has been dictated to him as a true copy of the current, frankly fascist aspects of current British monarchical strategic policy-shaping,

My repeated reference to the connection of those aspects of Obama's current health-care policy to that of the wartime Adolf Hitler, should not be considered as in any way either exaggerated, or egregious, or surprising. The shaping of Hitler's career as a Nazi, was as a Hitler who was also actually directed, as from above, by the influence on broad areas of social policy as also physical science practice, by British ideologues working from within the context of the positivist trends typified by Ernst Mach and the relatively, and savagely more radical Bertrand Russell.

The most well-known and notorious, later parts of Hitler's 1923-1945 career, had been set into motion, and largely sponsored, from the early 1920s, on, by the sponsorship which his political faction received, until the 1940 break, from such elements of the British ideological establishment as H.G. Wells and the British monarchy itself, while, similarly, the chief backing for Hitler's installation as Chancellor came through both the head of the Bank of England Montagu Norman, and Norman's agent within the Bank for International Settlements (BIS), Hjalmar Schacht. It was through Montagu Norman's partnership with Brown Brothers Harriman, that that latter firm's Prescott Bush, who is the father and grandfather, respectively, of two Bush Presidents, arranged a very special funding of the Nazi Party, a funding which was intended to put Hitler into power in Germany. This was done by the intention which

Prescott Bush shared with his business associate, the head of the Bank of England, Schacht-master Montagu Norman, at that time.

Thus, for those who know the relevant history of post-Versailles Germany, British-built Nazism was never a specifically German product; it was, essentially, a British-sponsored brand. Some mention of the post-1890 run-up into, during, and immediately following what is recalled as World War I, is crucial, ideologically, for understanding these sundry plots and connections.

This connection should never have been overlooked by anyone who knows the history and characteristics of the British Empire, either at its inception, in February 1763, or, still, today. The method by which the British East India Company had become the British Empire then, had been the so-called Seven Years War which had been orchestrated by the relevant British agencies, a war by means of which continental Europe ruined itself to that Company's great satisfaction. That is the kernel of the method by which British imperialism is perpetuated today, the method of religious warfare promoted among one's intended victims, as in the Near East, as that method had been presented to Lord Shelburne by the author of the **Decline and Fall of the Roman Empire**, Edward Gibbon.

For a similar case of the practice of the British Empire, still today, take the case of Britain's creating World War I as an echo of the method used by Britain to create the Seven Years War, and, today, what I have already referenced here as the case of the British royal consort, Prince Philip of World Wildlife Fund notoriety, for example.

A Factor of Brutishness in History

To understand how fraudulent schemes such as the doctrine of Lord Shelburne's agent Adam Smith, function, still today, against such intended victims such as the dupes currently dominating the policies of the U.S. government today, we need a glance at what is known as "populist" ideology.

The current British Royal Consort, Prince Philip of the populist "Bilderberger" mythology, is actually a flagrant advocate of the same brutal population and related, infamous policies which the relevant sort of right-wing populist, or rabid "environmentalist," shares with the Hitler regime's tradition, and also with the Prince's own reference to a relevant sort of personal family and kindred roots in continental Europe.

So, the admittedly foolish devotees of populist "con-necto" fantasies, have attempted to explain away what is today the highly relevant case of the real history of the Hitler phenomenon, and comparable cases, by resorting to purported explanations like those of assumed sorts of alleged histories, as if history itself were a Cartesian-like jig-saw puzzle premised on silly searches for some presumed one little pair of connected parts.[30]

As I have emphasized, repeatedly, since the opening of this present report, social processes in history are not Cartesian-like, but, as Leibniz warned, *dynamic,* or as Shelley emphasized what is actually the principle of dynamics in the concluding paragraph of his **A Defence of Poetry**. The cause of the process as a whole never originates in the parts, but directly the opposite. The part is moved, as in the case of the organization of our Solar system as a whole, by a principle like that of gravitation, by the influence of some subsuming, higher, unifying principles. This conception of the foundations of scientific method, is to be traced in history from the ideas of astronomy associated with ancient Sphaerics, and its principle of *dynamis*, which was adopted in ancient Europe from Egypt, through the Pythagoreans.

It is very important, in approaching the principal subject-matter of this present chapter, to emphasize that the typical way in which the case of the Bilderberger association has been popularly misrepresented in its role as a "conspiracy" in such an utterly silly fashion, is, clinically, essentially typical of the often mentally deranged, "bottom-up" varieties of the populist varieties of "conspiracy-mongering."

That fact of the matter is, that, the "Bilderbergers" association which was headed jointly by Britain's Philip and Prince Bernhard of the Netherlands, was the product, created from above, by a subsuming higher principle which governed those activities. That principle was that oligarchical principle of that British Empire which had its origin in the emergence of the so-called Liberal faction of Venice's Paolo Sarpi. Sarpi's imperial Liberalism, of which the Bilderbergers were an offshoot, was, in turn, a product of the long process expressed by that system of European imperialism, which is to be traced, among other developments, to the role of the Temple of Delphi in such cases as both the famous ruin of Croesus, and in the launching of the Peloponnesian War. That is typical of a true conspiratorial association; the association is a subsumed expression of a principle which governs the very existence of the ac-

---

30. E.g., Laplace's "three-body problem."

Social processes in history, LaRouche writes, are not Cartesian-like, but dynamic, as that concept was developed from the ancient Sphaerics *from Egypt, through the Pythagoreans. Here, Raphael's depiction of Pythagoras (center), in a detail from the "School of Athens."*

tivities of that association, from the top, down: not because the suspected hip-bone was connected to the alleged jaw. Such kaleidoscopically evolving successions of social systems among the credulous, organized in a top-down fashion by the witting, are the true empirical kernel of such processes in real history.

It is only through a top-down change in the line of descent of history, that really willful innovations in the chain of successive developments in society are, actually, willfully brought about. Thus, it has been the continuing existential conflict between the British empire and our republic which has been the pole of conflict across the Atlantic divide, and the greatest issue of principle throughout the world as a whole since February 1763. It was the polarity around which all general trends in world history have orbited since the developments in New England between 1620 and 1688-89, and still do today.

Thus, Prince Philip was not bad because he was caught confessing, however reluctantly, or not, to have slept with his wife, Queen Elizabeth, but because both were crucial in their temporary role as historically tran-

sitional figures in their relationship to the functioning of the ruling oligarchy of British empire. To call the Bilderbergers a "conspiracy" in the manner some populists do, is like accusing mice of inventing cheese.

What our populist "conspiracy mavens" are really trying to do, is to convince themselves, as anarchists or fascist ideologues would tend to do, that what has become today, that so poorly studied process which is actual history, is largely a hoax. The populists, for example, believe in a Cartesian fantasy-world, in which the isolated intentions of some individuals, not the dynamics of social processes, shape the course of what we saner fellows know as actually the intrinsically dynamic quality of the intellectual impetus operating within the social processes which are shaping real historical developments, shaping history as the movement of evolving ideas and themes over successive generations. It is not the figures being played on the apparent political chessboard, but the real players, like the fellows playing the chess game of *Kriegspiel* against one another, who play the game, not as a simple conspiracy, but as a playing out of yet another, new evolution in their approach to what passes for the accumulated experience of the evolution of the standpoint from which two really dedicated chess players play out yet a new round of a game of chess. It is the evolution of the standards of play in the leading examples of the competitions, which defines the game as played.

Or, in summary of our attention to this important point: to report the same thing in a more efficient way, the pro-anarchoid type of the populist, rejects the concept of dynamics, and, therefore, could never recognize the poetry of Percy Bysshe Shelley, or any other work of Classical artistic composition, as properly intelligible.

Therefore, do not be so silly as to make deductions from Smith's arguments. Study his virtually "pre-programmed" sort of mind, as that is to be seen in a way which is shown most clearly, as a kind of confession of stupidity, in his **Theory of Moral Sentiments**. Study him as one would study a variety of bug, focussing on the way the bug's mind works, rather than what he presents to us as his conclusions. Focus on his mind in the way a skilled hunter anticipates the movements and other behavior of his intended prey.

Do not be fooled by what Smith says; rather, observe that, so to speak, as I shall make the point here, that the flap in his "Dr. Dentons" is down.

Consider a most relevant excerpt from Smith's **Theory of the Moral Sentiments**, as follows:

"[though we are] endowed with a very strong desire of those ends, it has not been intrusted to the slow and uncertain determinations of our reason, to find out the proper means of bringing them about, Nature has directed us to the greater part of these by original and immediate instincts. Hunger, thirst, the passion which unites the two sexes, the love of pleasure, and the dread of pain, prompt us to apply those means for their own sakes, and without any consideration of their tendency to those beneficent ends which the great Director of nature intended to produce by them."

Relative to that more subtle Dr. François Quesnay, who was the relevant predecessor of Adam Smith, Smith was a crude lout of the sort one might imagine as teaching his fledgling son the family business of organized crime. Nonetheless, despite a certain difference in quality of mind between the two, what is presented by Smith, in the passage I have excerpted for this purpose, is a faithful echo of what, shall we say, "Smith is attempting to say."

I have brought both this excerpt, and the related matter of Quesnay into play here, to emphasize a crucially indicative feature, and also a certain historically significant point of difference between Quesnay and that passage from Smith.

Smith says, in effect: "You, man, are just another animal, a pre-programmed beast, with the added feature of special bestialities." The crucially indicative feature of that text, is the passage, "without any consideration of their tendency to those beneficent ends which the great Director of nature intended to produce by them." He lies.

We should recognize an echo of the spirit of Smith on this account, in H.G. Wells' **The Island of Dr. Moreau.**

Directly contrary to Smith, all mankind is crucially distinguished from all beasts, by that power of reason which is expressed in a relatively simplest, but nonetheless conclusive way; we make discoveries of principle to such an effect, that if something comparable to that appeared in a relatively lower form of life, we should consider that as, at least, presenting us with an improved variety of the species, or, even a new species, that by virtue of the changes in capacity shown as the qualitative change of capability in what had seemed to be a mere change in the antecedent varieties' behavior.

It is the essence of a competent study of economic processes, that these qualitative changes in capacity, in human behavior, have an ordered quality. When viewed in retrospect, we call an ordered succession of this class as showing a direction to which we attach the notion of "progress." In general, the idea of "progress" is to be measured as an increase of the potential relative population-density of the human species, per capita, and per relative unit of potential relative population-density, a cultural change. That is a form of development which does not exist within the bounds of the working definition of a species of a lower form of life.

This directed character of the distinction between both man and beast, and human progress or retrogression, supplies us experimental proof of the existence of the knowable intention expressed as what Smith terms the "Great Director of Nature." Mankind's culturally upward-evolutionary development, in this sense, expresses that intention which Smith has denied to exist.

Therefore, for reason of what is typified by that argument by Smith, actual morality does not exist among true Liberals, but only currently reigning customs, as the cases of President Obama's behaviorist ideologues illustrate the specific immorality of modern Liberalism, as, similarly, the British launching of Adolf Hitler did.

Now, that said, look backwards, from Smith, to Dr. Quesnay.

It is interesting, therefore, that Quesnay, contrary to the putative atheist Smith, believes in a knowable type of sympathetic magic, this feature of the French background of British ideology which excited Karl Marx the most. In some ways, the more customary entertainments of Deer Park put aside, Quesnay is quite religious, if only in his own fashion. He believes that the grant of a paper conferring a title of nobility upon the proprietor of a feudal estate, is the sole, essentially magical source of the increment of wealth realized by that estate. The farmers employed upon that estate possess, for him, the economic significance of a special breed of cattle. That is the essential social principle of his *Tableau economique, the principle which Marx parodies in his efforts to make the lunacy of British Liberalism appear rational.* Marx admires British economics otherwise, because he perceives it to be outwardly successful, to such a degree that only an aberrant descendant of the British system could be what Marx foresees as a hereditary successor-form of economy.[31]

---

31. Karl Marx did tend to be drawn to admiration of the United States, but British agent Frederick Engels managed, repeatedly, to put a stop to that, as, for example, in Marx's soon-corrected admiration of some of

Otherwise, Quesnay tends to honor living processes, if not actual human beings, even that only at the level of what Vernadsky identifies as the Biosphere, and that only by a broad choice of implication. Quesnay's additional marginal advantage over Smith is that he adopts the standpoint of agricultural production, whereas Smith is fully occupied, like his accomplice, Jeremy Bentham, in stealing the English ruling and middle classes' consumption from the fruits of labor, as the George W. Bush, Jr., administration did, and the Obama administration has been doing, even more lavishly, thus far.

Now, contrast these Eighteenth-century empiricists with the actually scientific outlook familiar to us over a span from the Pythagoreans such as Archytas, through Plato, Eratosthenes, Brunelleschi, Cusa, Leonardo, Kepler, Fermat, Leibniz, and so on. In all these and comparable cases, the intention of the Creator, is the creation of higher states of existence in our universe, especially human existence, as this notion is famously expressed in the work of Leibniz and such of his followers through Riemann, Einstein, and Vernadsky. In all these cases, man is exerting increasing power within the universe. There lies the manifest intention of mankind's existence.

As LaRouche presented in a 1988 television commentary, "The Woman on Mars," had we continued what we had begun with the Moon landing, "we could have put a woman, by now, into the leadership of a temporary mission-assignment on that planet." Shown: Mars, as seen by the Hubble Space Telescope.

Our Creatures of Prometheus

Primarily, our contemporary, anti-nuclear fanatics are proponents of a type of presently dying economy, as in President Obama's administration so far, which is being transformed today, under President Obama's current policy, into what is currently designed to transform our nation into a green and dying corpse. The agency of our republic's thus-intended self-destruction, is a modern echo of the pro-Satanic cult which is traced, in globally extended European history, to the ban on human creativity by the frankly Satanic Olympian Zeus of the **Prometheus** story, a ban by the cult of Apollo, and, most

---

the work of Henry C. Carey.

emphatically, by the terrorist legacy of that anarchist, ancient, city-burners' cult of Dionysus which is also characteristic of the fruits of the "68er" cult today.

The characteristic of all systemic expressions of evil in known history, has been, in principle, the denial of the existence of, or, in the alternative, a prohibition against that same principle which Aeschylus' **Prometheus Bound** identifies as a principle of "fire," such as nuclear power today. This evil, Dionysian legacy of the Delphi cult, as we observed it emerging to its present, virulent form during the period leading into the uproar of 1968, is, as the Luddites of the early Nineteenth Century were, and the degenerates known as the "greenies" today. It is a calculated rebirth of the cult of Dionysus, through the influence of frankly pro-satanic circles identified with figures such as Aleister Crowley, H.G. Wells, and Bertrand Russell. The objective for which this moral degeneration was fomented, is merely typified by Prince Philip's backing of the frankly pro-Satanic World Wildlife Fund.

The destiny of the world at large, and, therefore, also our republic lies in freeing ourselves from everything which even smells of the present British imperial system. To do that, we must now reach a wee bit higher than economists have even imagined before.

V. The Next Stop, Mars

To deal effectively with the world-wide, and yet more distant realities of today, we must look at economy from the standpoint of dynamics, looking at this from the neighboring vantage-point which is our own galaxy as a whole, and continuing on down to Earth, not the customary, other way around. We must regard the special nature of our human species, by seeing our species and its future mission within that galaxy; and, then, that oncoming role of man within it all, from that standpoint, in that future, now.

Mankind's existence itself should not be cramped

in the confines of Earth in that manner which today's customary views suggest. Admittedly, the minds of governments are now cramped within the confines of a memory of what has outlived its time, and are confined by certain habits which, in the main, are not worthy to repeat. We must abandon the foolishness of these recent times. We must look to the heavens, to our Solar system as the most immediate part of this galaxy, and, then, look down toward our selves, as we might be seen from above, in this process, from the future, until today. Look back from the future to both our present and our past, toward a new intended destiny. It is a future, coming up toward us, from a reference-point above the Solar system as a whole, or our galaxy, beyond.[32]

Perhaps, but only perhaps, it is regrettable, that, perhaps, none of us from my own or the later generation of today, shall live long enough to see the foot of our Earthly species touch upon the planets of other parts of the Solar system, beyond our Moon, a destiny reserved, today, for younger generations.

As I summarized the facts of the matter in that television documentary published widely in 1988, now more than twenty years ago, **The Woman on Mars**, what we had begun with the Moon landing, could have put a woman, by now, into the leadership of a temporary mission-assignment on that planet. It would have been a mission-assignment to visit a crafted scientific-experimental base on Mars. It would be in a fashion similar to the work of those scientists who have been working, on temporary assignments, in Antarctica, dwelling for a time within habitats used by successive teams. Our regrets for what did not happen as I had hoped in 1988, notwithstanding, mankind may prepare, again, to travel in that direction now, still, but, probably, only through a fresh grasp of what has become a lost sense of the immortality of that higher mission to which we should now foresee mankind committed, soon. We must find, thus, the true meaning of the limits of our own lives, not in dying, but in the immortal, higher missions in which we shall continue to be a part, that through a vision of the way we should have lived, without regrets, today.

The greatest minds and souls of science, and of art, from our present past, have lived their lives in just that way. True science has always been like that, for as far back as we can know. If, now, in a presently evil time, of the present British health-care policy, of mass-killings of the lovable by the despicable, we can come to see ourselves in such a fresh new way, then, there is hope, that we, too, could grasp the true meaning of our living now, and rejoice again, as the great minds have done before us, in devotion to what the future of mankind might still become, today.

Keeping this in mind, what I have just stated, in opening this present chapter, should prompt us to consider the true meaning lodged, as if behind that cheating mask which had become the present ideology of most among those who occupy high places now, to see that which is to be seen in a proper comprehension of the principles of my science of physical economy.

If you think today, that you are mystified by any of what I have just written here, above, let me clarify that now for you. It is important to you, in fact, that you know exactly what I have to say on that account, here, and now. You should consider these to be the most essential, if only rather elementary truths, the true secrets of that presently oncoming role of a science of physical economy on which the rescue of our ruined civilization, now, immediately depends.

Vernadsky's Universe

Modern science reached a certain point, after Gauss, with Bernhard Riemann, and then with Albert Einstein. Then came Russia's Academician V.I. Vernadsky, the scientist who rediscovered life.[33] Vernadsky actually developed a competent notion of physical biochemistry,[34] but then, also, showed, in similar ways, that human life in the Noösphere is a higher form of universal existence than mere life by itself. As I have already referenced this in sharing earlier portions of this present report, we know, largely because of him, of three distinct states of being, constituting, thus, three phase-spaces of the known universe, each separated

---

32. In true science, it has been clearly understood for more than century, now, that time by itself, as if it were a dimension independent of the rest, such as space or matter, does not exist.

33. Although, of course, Vernadsky died first.

34. Compare, and contrast Vernadsky's discoveries, on this account, with the views expressed by the Soviet scientist A.I. Oparin and the Oparin-Haldane thesis. Although V.I. Vernadsky adopted the term "Noösphere" from hearing the term from Teilhard de Chardin, there is no ontological coherence between the use of the term by Chardin and that of Vernadsky. The worst perversion of the notion of life is that radically reductionist notion of mere "complexity," which was derived from such followers of Bertrand Russell as those associated with the cultish followers of Professor Norbert Wiener at MIT's RLE, John von Neumann, and the mystics of Silicon Valley.

from the other by the occurrence of a definite and unique, universal principle, as Johannes Kepler's uniquely original discovery of the universal principle of gravitation supplies a model for that distinction.

That is to say, that human life, which appears in the context of life generally, defines an added, unique principle which is, ontologically, categorically distinct from both the abiotic and biotic domains. He defines our experience, as we know it from facts of experimental science, as the specific quality of the Noösphere.

What I have introduced as a crucial premise of a science of physical economy, as I have stated in earlier sections of this report, has given us the notion of the relationship among these three, qualitatively distinct physical states, of that which is, respectively, not life, life, and the universally efficient, physical principle of the creative phases of the human intellect. The distinct quality of intellect, provides a method of organization of the experimental evidence to show an ordered succession of nested states of existence, such that the biotic domain encloses, with its expressed development, the abiotic, and the Biosphere is enclosed, within the Noösphere. The significance of that for our discussion, here, is that the Noösphere encloses the universe insofar as we know that universe experimentally, up to the present stage of related developments.

The general principle upon which this notion of the Noösphere depends, coincides, for me, with that principle which I adopted, in 1953, from reflection, then, on the implications of Bernhard Riemann's 1854 habilitation dissertation. I so defined a physical science of economy, in that time. This has served me as the basis for my successful economic forecasting, since 1956 to the present day.

Most notable, among the practical implications of my adoption of a Riemannian approach to analysis of physical-economic processes, was that it urged me to downgrade the relative scientific authority of widely employed, merely statistical notions of economic value, such as those of the British school generally, and the included case of Marxian economy. In fact, during several decades since my Summer 1956 forecast of the outbreak of the 1957-58 U.S. deep recession, I have, customarily, "back-translated" what I knew from a Riemannian standpoint, into what passed among professionals, and others, generally at that time, for what can be fairly described as conventional British Liberal, or Marxian terms.

In the meantime, as in my very brief, passing correspondence with the economist Wassily Leontief, in the late 1950s, I expressed my sense of the need to rid the practice of economics from the wildly reductionist, but growing, pathological influence of Bertrand Russell, and his clone John von Neumann, from among what Leontief, among some others regarded, as I did, as a depraved, "ivory-tower" cult of mathematical economists. This debate intersected, and overlapped my chief frustration as a working economist, my frustration with the customary limitations of "linearization," which was the remaining shortfall of the otherwise excellent work of Leontief in his contributions to the crafting of the U.S.A.'s own national-income accounting system.

Those limitations precluded the kind of forecasting system needed to judge the qualitative impact of scientifically crucial changes in technology, even the probable impact of the emergence of the foreseeable use of computer technology, increasingly, as a potential factor of "non-linear," qualitative change in the day-to-day management of the economy in the main.[35] The methods of the "ivory tower" school, on which Leontief and I shared the wisp of a very brief like-minded moment, in opposition to the utopians, were worthless for such an undertaking; the exchange was important for me, because his brief reply itself, prompted me to break free, then, from the remaining shackles of conventional practice, shackles such as those of the mental prison of "linear programming." My activity as a long-range forecaster, through the present time, had come about as a result of my accumulation of such scientific concerns, and related developments, over the time since the mid-1950s.

Two decades later, my continued concentration on explicitly Riemannian approaches, as prompted by the aftermath of my success in the 1971 Queens College debate with Professor Abba Lerner, led me from a sequence of my fair and decent writings presenting popularizable by-products of my views, to such qualitative outbursts of protest against the pompous yahoos of that time, as were expressed by my "Poetry Must Supersede Mathematics in Economics." By that time, for reason of my increasingly impassioned preoccupation with the subject of creativity as such, I had become, increasingly, occupied by the process of becoming, more and

------

35. What should be readily recognized as this effect of computer technology, includes the impact of the several factors of time, such as the contrast between simple lapsed time, and reaction-time affecting a change in the quality of a relevant physical process.

more, a committed advocate of the application of certain leading work by Academician Vernadsky, for redefining the principles of physical economy.

Those developments in current history, have lately reached the present point of world crisis, in which the entire planetary system of economic thinking must, in any eventuality, be suddenly, and radically changed. The present global situation is such, that nothing good on this planet is generally possible, unless this change is made. We have thus, in this fashion, entered a certain unique period of calamity of the world economy as a whole, a point comparable to the eve of the great ecumenical Council of Florence, when unfamiliarity with a remedy, is no longer a decent excuse for avoiding it.

The Remedy

As I have conceded here earlier, the use of money and its prices, is largely unavoidable for the purposes of exchanges in the small. However, rather than being considered, any longer, as a determinant of economic value, money itself should converge on the far more modest task of serving as an assigned standard for methods of pricing of exchanges within the ranges of the small. It is not a measure of economic value, but a convenient assignment of apparent value for the purpose of freeing us from tasks which do not matter when processes are considered in the large.

True economic value in the large, lies in the effect of today's consumption on the future potential relative population-density of the society. This is a functionally determined physical value, measured in terms of the concept of relevant increases and decreases of a society's potential relative population-density, rather than a monetary, or comparable function in the large. Any system of pricing employed should reflect that distinction, in effect.

The notions which I have just presented, thus, are expressions of physical potential, which is defined, in turn, as Gottfried Leibniz defined *dynamics* during the beginning of his treatment of that subject, in his attacks on the frauds of Rene Descartes during the 1690s. Strictly speaking, the term *dynamics*, so employed, implies what became the notion of the *tensor* as defined in physical terms, after the relevant work of Gauss, from the point of reference of Bernhard Riemann's contributions, and, to be fussy about it all, an integrated view of Vernadsky's definitions of the respective abiotic, Biosphere, and Noösphere domains.

As a matter of real current practice in the real social processes of economy, it is generally sufficient, still today, that such notions be employed heuristically, as guides to judgments, rather than demanding more exact scrutiny. The crucial implications of estimates employed, are to be located in the effects of science-driven technological progress, as combined, for consideration, with the factors of capital-intensity over their span of useful life. Clearly, the determination of relative value, especially in cases of long-term, capital-intense investments, depends upon the manner and degree of the use of that investment, as much as the potential represented by its existence.

However, the immediately foregoing discussion is merely background, intended to impart a sense of the gist of the matter; the crucial considerations are of a different nature, as follows.

The increase of the effective potential relative population-density of human population, is broadly indicated by a process through which the Biosphere is increased as a portion of the mass of the planet, relative to that of the non-living aspect of the planet. For this purpose, the Biosphere is defined not only as "living matter," but also forms of dead matter which have come into existence as specifically by-products of living human and other processes. Thus, in this way, as the population of living processes increases, and also increases its productivity per capita and per square kilometer, the rate of change (increase) of the Biosphere increases relative to the abiotic aspect of the planet. A comparable, but different quality of relationship, but to comparable effect, occurs in the Biosphere's development and continued activity generally. Comparably, the increase of the Noösphere's number of individuals and their aggregate mass, occurs as a relative diminishing of the ratio of the Biosphere to the Noösphere, although the ratio of the Biosphere to the abiotic is increasing, and that necessarily.

As the Biosphere's relative development in and for itself, requires the development of a more powerful dynamic mass of the components of the Biosphere as a whole, so the development of the physical productive powers of labor per capita and per square kilometer, requires a higher degree of the intellectual productive power of mankind, per capita, and an increase of the rate of growth of relative capital-intensity.

In that broadly described pattern, the power of the living processes (the Biosphere) is increased relative to the mass of our planet, and the increased productivity of mankind per capita, and per square kilometer of the

Earth's surface, must increase relative to the rate of increase of the Biosphere.

So, as I have pointed out earlier, the inorganic aspect of the Earth does not contain the Biosphere, but directly the opposite; whereas, the human population is not a subsumed outcome of the Biosphere as a process. Rather, the Biosphere as a process, contains the Earth's abiotic existence, and the Noösphere's contains the Biosphere.

Furthermore, contrary to the reductionists, the modern reductionists most emphatically, the action of both the Biosphere and Noösphere are each, respectively anti-entropic, although in relatively different modes. In short, the creative powers of the individual human mind, so summarily described, are the expression of the highest power, as measured in projected rate of change, both within our planet, and, implicitly, of our planet within the Solar system today.

The so-called "law of universal entropy," as implied in the argument by Rudolf Clausius and Hermann Grassmann, is a lie, and a hoax.

As shocking as that may seem to some, it is mild when compared with a higher, more powerful truth. The most powerful forces for change on our planet are of the ontological character of the Leibniz "infinitesimal." The reality of what is expressed as that infinitesimal, is expressed by Nicholas of Cusa's exposure of the hoax of the notion of the quadrature of the circle, by Kepler's related discovery of the Earth's orbit, and, even more emphatically, in his later discovery of the principle of universal gravitation, in his **The Harmonies of the World**.

What those ironies combine to show, is that our sense-perceptions are not reality, but are the shadows cast by an unseen reality upon our sense-perceptual apparatus. The apparently shadowy effects expressed as the relevant, nominally "infinitesimal forces," express the reality which sense-perception can not analyze, but which are the expression of the powerful realities for which sense-perception is merely a shadow.

Here, in what seems to many, wrongly, as the domain of innuendo, dwells the creativity expressed in such forms as the ironies of which effective Classical poetry is composed. There is, of course, a distinction between truthful such innuendo and the counterfeit. It is that truthful innuendo, such as that of Classical poetry,

Up until now, under the influence of such as Prince Philip, the U.S. has destroyed itself, "for the pleasure of the Union Jerk."

"If mankind is to reach the stars, that is the thought, in memory of the like of our great hero President Franklin Roosevelt, which you must now remember."

which reflects the powers which moved the real world of John Keats and Percy Bysshe Shelley. It is the same with the work of Johann Sebastian Bach. It is within the domain of great Classical expressions of art, that the power which moves physical science lurks, ready to strike. Such is the creative power whose shadow is that which moves and creates the universe.

Such is the true dignity of mankind.

This brings us to the final, most immediately crucial of the issues which have been selected to be treated in intended conclusion of this report thus far.

How London Has Ruined Us This Far

Up to the moment of the death of President Franklin Roosevelt, on April 12, 1945, the intention of our United States had been to bring down the British Empire, at long last, in order to free the world from imperialism through the political liberation and promoted economic self-development of the empire's direct, and indirect prey. As I have noted at the outset of this report, President Roosevelt's successor, Harry S Truman, showed his hand as a British lackey within moments of the news of Franklin Roosevelt's death.

As I have said here earlier, instead of using the vast productive potential which our republic had developed for both the recovery of the U.S. economy from the ravages of the Coolidge and Hoover administrations, and for the mission of liberating the post-war world from the effects of British tyranny, the actions of the Truman administration intentionally ruined a vast portion of that potential which war had bequeathed to a post-war world. Truman proved himself promptly a lackey of the imperial forces represented, typically, by those British and U.S. financier circles which had combined forces to place fascist regimes such as those of Mussolini and Hitler in place over the course of the 1920s and 1930s. As Churchill's fraudulent declaration of an "Iron Curtain," and peace-lover Bertrand Russell's declaration of preventive nuclear war against a nation without such weapons, set the pace, the freeing of colonies was "off the table," and a new form of imperialism was launched from places including the U.S.A. and Britain, by those financier and associated circles who had been the creators of the fascism of the 1920s, the 1930s, and the just concluded general war.

That, however, was, by no means, the limit of the crime in which President Truman was complicit. The post-war intention of the British Empire and its lackeys within the financier establishment of our United States, was, chiefly, ultimately, to destroy and assimilate our United States itself. Many means were employed to kindred such ends, but, above all others, the principal goal of the British empire and its treasonous assets within our ranks, was to destroy our character and the vast economic power which had been our United States.

To this end, a long wave of neo-Malthusian impulses was implanted among us, and within that continent of Europe which was yearning to rebuild itself from the ravages of fascism and war. Hitler was dead in those times, but what the British Empire had created in that Hitler, was working to kindred ends again. After all, the British Empire had always been the mother goddess of fascism globally, from the time of Lord Palmerston's Napoleon III, through the assassination of France's President Sadi Carnot, and the creation, by London, of the likes of Mussolini and Hitler, with help of the likes of Wall Street, after the close of the first great world war.

The British Empire has pretended still today, to be our friend, but it has always been, at the same time, our republic's only ultimate, eternal enemy. Our republic's chief enemy, abroad and from within, has been the fools who have refused to see this essential truth.

The particular expression of what is tantamount to political and economic stupidity, on this account, polluting the political ranks of even our own self-esteemed patriots, is their cultivated ignorance of the essential principle of all human civilized history. The form of that mass-stupidity reaching into the circles of even leading parts of our citizenry, can be identified, systemically, as the influence of that particular form of induced cultural derangement which is typified by the methods of Cartesian reductionism, as distinct from the more efficient patriot's devotion to the tradition of Leibniz's notion of dynamics. Those citizens who are corrupted, reflect the fact, that they think in the small, almost like neighborhood gossips, rather than thinking men and women. Like a boiled frog, they have seen the prey before their nose, but not the fact that they are being cooked.

So, inch by inch, the legacy of Franklin Roosevelt's rescue of our republic, was cooked by the methods of British Liberalism's influence upon the practices of our economy, and by the destruction of the morals-in-the-large of our influential circles of government and economic policy-shaping affairs. The assassination of President Kennedy, points to the same circles operating then from within the Spanish-speaking world which were engaged in the attempted killing of France's President de Gaulle, which remain the chief real suspects for what came across the border with Mexico on that evil occasion. The motive for the killing lay in the exemplary case of the Wall Street gang's steel bosses, and, more emphatically, in President Kennedy's decision, based in part on the advice of Generals MacArthur and Eisenhower, not to plunge the U.S.A. into a disastrous "land war in Asia," then, as in the folly of the wasting of our troops again, under President Obama, in Afghanistan today.

In short, the most evil man of the Twentieth Century, more evil, in the longer run, than even the Hitler created by the British Empire for the purpose of yet-another "Seven Years War," has been Bertrand Russell. Hitler was monstrously evil, but it is British so-called pacifists like Russell, and his worshipful dupes, who make the catastrophes which serve the really long-term interests of the Devil himself.

It has been under the influence of the Bertrand Russell who preceded Prince Philip in such crimes, that we of our United States have foolishly, like a boiled frog, destroyed ourselves for the pleasure of the Union Jerk.

If mankind is to reach the stars, that is the thought, in memory of the like of our great hero, President Franklin Roosevelt, which you must now remember.

Appendix

'A Defence of Poetry'

From the essay thus-named by Percy Bysshe Shelley (1792-1822):

[W]e live among such philosophers and poets as surpass beyond comparison any who have appeared since the last national struggle for civil and religious liberty. The most unfailing herald, companion, and follower of the awakening of a great people to work a beneficial change in opinion or institution, is poetry. At such periods, there is an accumulation of the power of communicating and receiving profound and impassioned conceptions respecting man and nature. The persons in whom this power resides, may often, as far as regards many portions of their nature, have little apparent correspondence with that spirit of good of which they are the ministers. But even whilst they deny and abjure, they are yet compelled to serve, the power which is seated upon the throne of their own soul. It is impossible to read the compositions of the most celebrated writers of the present day without being startled with the electric life which burns within their words. They measure the circumference and sound the depths of human nature with a comprehensive and all-penetrating spirit, and they are themselves perhaps the most sincerely astonished at its manifestations: for it is less their spirit than the spirit of the age.

FIDELIO

Journal of Poetry, Science, and Statecraft

From the first issue, dated Winter 1992, featuring Lyndon LaRouche on "The Science of Music: The Solution to Plato's Paradox of 'The One and the Many,'" to the final issue of Spring/Summer 2006, a "Symposium on Edgar Allan Poe and the Spirit of the American Revolution," *Fidelio* magazine gave voice to the Schiller Institute's intention to create a new Golden Renaissance.

The title of the magazine, is taken from Beethoven's great opera, which celebrates the struggle for political freedom over tyranny. *Fidelio* was founded at the time that LaRouche and several of his close associates were unjustly imprisoned, as was the opera's Florestan, whose character was based on the American Revolutionary hero, the French General, Marquis de Lafayette.

Each issue of *Fidelio*, throughout its 14-year lifespan, remained faithful to its initial commitment, and offered original writings by LaRouche and his associates, on matters of, what the poet Percy Byssche Shelley identified as, "profound and impassioned conceptions respecting man and nature."

Back issues are now available for purchase through the Schiller Institute website:
http://schillerinstitute.org/about/order_form.html